The Easy Way to CHINESE COOKING

The
Easy
Way
to

CHINESE COOKING

by Beverly Lee

WITH ILLUSTRATIONS BY HERBERT MARK

DOUBLEDAY & COMPANY, INC., GARDEN CITY, NEW YORK

LIBRARY OF CONGRESS CATALOG CARD NUMBER 63–12982

PRINTED IN THE UNITED STATES OF AMERICA

To
UNCLE TERRY
who revolutionized my kitchen

ACKNOWLEDGMENTS

I am grateful to Carol Kraichnan for her unstinting moral support as well as her assistance in helping me test recipes, to Elliot Schryver for his time and efforts in helping me organize my thoughts and the text, and to my dear husband who was so nice about having his meals late or in shifts, and who never seemed to mind eating the same dish several nights in a row.

CONTENTS

INTRODUCTION   1

BASIC UTENSILS FOR CHINESE COOKING   4

Chinese utensils — acceptable American substitutes — how to care for them

INGREDIENTS   10

Basic ingredients — Chinese vegetables, dried goods, sauces, dried and powdered herbs and spices, other seasonings, noodles and wrappers, miscellaneous — their uses and how to store them

SCHOOLS OF COOKING AND METHODS OF PREPARATION   40

How to slice, shred, dice, and chop for Chinese cooking methods

MASTERING THE METHOD OF CHOW   48

Principles and goals of stir frying — organizing one's kitchen for chow — finer techniques of using the wok — recipes, from one ingredient to authentic Chinese combinations — what the finished dish should look like — Western versions

MASTERING THE METHOD OF JING   99

Principles and goals of steaming — Chinese utensils and Western substitutes — advantages of steaming — recipes

MASTERING THE METHOD OF RED COOKING   114

How to red stew and roast — advantages of red cooking — recipes

NOODLES   122

RICE   133

How to make proper boiled rice — types of raw rice — recipes

SOUPS   141

WHAT TO DRINK   145

Wines — teas

DESSERTS   149

How to end a Chinese meal

RECIPES USING OTHER COOKING METHODS   152

MENU PLANNING   163

Suggested menus for 4 and 6 people — how to give a Chinese dinner party for 8 to 16 people

MARKETS WHERE CHINESE INGREDIENTS   169
MAY BE PURCHASED

INDEX   171

The
Easy
Way
to CHINESE COOKING

INTRODUCTION

For several years now I have been teaching Chinese cooking at the China Institute in New York City. In my experiences as a cooking instructor, I've noticed that the interest in food—not merely Chinese food, but food in general—has increased tremendously. One reason is that help has become virtually nonexistent in our middle-class way of life. The housewife does the cooking and has grown tired of standard fare. Some have come to recognize that cooking is truly the one creative part of a homemaker's life and preparing a meal is her way of expressing love for her family, so, if one must eat, why not enjoy it?

My classes are composed of different types of people. There is the type who is just plain bored with her everyday existence and is really searching for something different to talk about. She usually turns out to be an observer, strictly a spectator, and would be horrified at the thought of getting her hands dirty. I remember one woman, standing and watching the rest of the class, who said in a very imperious tone to the person standing next to her, "I can't even boil water." Evidently she was proud of this rather dubious achievement. Then there is the enthusiast, usually a career girl, who is taking the course because she just plain doesn't know how to cook. This person at first is very awkward and self-conscious but eventually is carried away by her enthusiasm and, before the course is over, is eagerly telling me about her successful dinner party for which, of course, the food was all Chinese and all cooked by her. She probably gets the most out of my classes, as far as basic knowledge of cooking goes.

The tea-party type—usually a housewife—jabbers incessantly during the demonstration and lecture and then doesn't know which end is up. By the end of the course, however, she has somehow managed to absorb something so all is not lost. Then there is the professional homemaker who has indeed discovered the joy of cooking as a creative art. She is self-assured, composed, at home with all the unusual kitchen utensils, capable of absorbing the entire course and adapting it to her home. She and the last type, the gourmet, who usually turns out to be a man, are a joy to have in the class.

Incidentally, I agree with all that has been written about the great chefs of the world being men, because I see time and time again that the men in my classes prove to be superior students. I feel that there is a good reason for this: the majority of the women of today look upon cooking as a necessity, something that has to be done and gotten out of the way. They are, after all, saddled with preparing three meals a day, and their meals show it. It is indeed the rare woman who has sublimated her creative instincts into the kitchen and discovered what untold joys she can gain for herself and her loved ones.

Through the years I have discovered that even a woman who is a rank beginner can become a whiz in the kitchen, for the woman who is constantly chattering about how bored she is with cooking and the kitchen is doing so for several reasons. She cannot cook and is afraid of failure. She is covering up her inadequacies by claiming a disinterest in food. No one is interested in doing something she cannot do well or knows nothing about. But given a little knowledge and a few basic principles, a woman's interest in food will come naturally. She will turn from a lamb to a tiger in the kitchen. It's all a matter of building up her self-confidence. Once she is armed with the proper knowledge, the interest will come and, along with that, compliments from her husband.

In all fairness, I should mention the important element of time. No one enjoys doing anything when lack of time plus distractions and interruptions are inevitable and, unfortunately, this is the lot of the busy mother. However, I feel that with a little planning and, of course, some knowledge, this can be overcome.

I think cooking, like any other thing, is a matter of knowing the basic principles and of being able to apply them in any given situation, whether it be Chinese, American, or Turkish.

In this book I hope to give the basic principles and techniques involved in Chinese cooking, along with appropriate recipes. But if the reader becomes a slave to the recipes then the point of the book will have been lost.

I have observed in my classes that the person who really gets her money's worth is the housewife who comes with the attitude that she is going to learn principles which she will then take home and adapt to *her* kitchen and *her* favorite vegetables and meats. I have had as students several rabbis' wives who, because of their rigid dietary rules, could not prepare over half of the recipes that I demonstrated but who did apply, with great success I am told, what they observed in the classroom to what was acceptable in their kitchens.

BASIC UTENSILS FOR CHINESE COOKING

A well-equipped Chinese kitchen has a *wok*. A wok is an iron pan with a round bottom. Aluminun ones are also available in large cities such as New York. The round bottom of the wok serves many purposes. It concentrates heat. There are no corners to hinder removal of food or to accumulate grease. It is economical, as it requires less oil than a conventional frying pan, and food cooked this way is less greasy and more palatable.

Wok

A deep cover and metal ring or base accompany the wok. The ring usually has several openings cut out but will require considerably more notches for an efficient flame. The notches can be made with a wire cutter. In the case of an electric burner, this would of course be unnecessary, but gas burners are much more suited to Chinese cooking, as they provide the instantaneous control of temperatures which is so important with this method of cooking. This does not mean that if you have an electric stove you should stop reading at this point—it just takes a bit more concentration and effort.

Woks come in various sizes and are classified according to the diameter of the rim of the pan. They range anywhere from 10 inches to 32 inches, which is the size used in restaurants. It should be kept in mind that the larger the wok the more difficult it is to get concentrated heat on a conventional range. Restaurants can achieve incredible temperatures because their ranges have wells strictly tailored for the wok with the flame surrounding the pan rather than the pan sitting on top of the flame as it does in an average kitchen. I own two woks, one twelve-inch and one sixteen-inch, but for the average-size family a fourteen-inch wok will be quite adequate.

One can easily substitute all the equipment mentioned with a frying pan (definitely an iron skillet) ten inches in diameter and three inches deep with a tight lid. As a matter of fact,

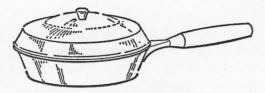

Frying Pan with Lid

I went without a wok for the longest time, and to this day my mother-in-law, who is a marvelous Chinese cook, does not own one.

There are two kitchen utensils which are specifically tailored for the wok. These are the *siou hok*, a round ladle-like utensil, and the *wok chan*, which is a flat turner. Both are used simultaneously since, in order to achieve a perfect chow dish, such high temperatures are required to seal in natural flavors and preserve texture that the utmost speed in stirring is necessary to prevent the ingredients from burning. The siou hok, or ladle, is held in the left hand and the wok chan in the right

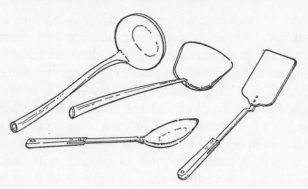

The *siou hok* and *wok chan*, with substitutes

hand. The actual stirring motion is a circular lifting and drop-
ping, like tossing a salad, to prevent bruising of ingredients. A
large metal spoon and a pancake turner approximately four
inches wide at the blade and three inches deep can be used
instead.

Speaking of the speed that is needed conjures up in my
mind the picture of a typical student in my class. After watching the demonstration of chow she attempts with great trepi-
dation to cook her first dish. She is usually as nervous as an
actress on opening night. Her motions are quick and jerky and
she manages to get some of the ingredients on the range top
rather than in the pan. By the second lesson she is less jittery
and by the third she is a self-assured old trouper. Which goes
to prove that it is simply a matter of practice.

If one does get a wok, however, it should be treated like an
iron frying pan; that is, it should be seasoned and, once seasoned, should never be scoured with any metal cleanser or
strong cleaning powders.

There are two ways of seasoning a wok. First coat the wok
with vegetable oil; then either bake it at a high temperature
or place it on a burner with a high flame and burn it. Which-
ever method is used—or for that matter a combination of both
can be used—persistence is important, as it will require sev-

Chow—first position

Chow—second position—"The Salad Toss"

eral "treatments" (and a strong exhaust fan) before the bottom is ready for use. After each treatment the excess oil which has burned and caked should be scoured off; it will eventually come off, and better now than later in the gravy of a prepared dish.

By seasoning the wok with vegetable oil, one seals the pores of the metal and prevents the sticking of food, a metallic flavor, and smarting of one's eyes. When the bottom of the pan is black, the pan is ready for use. Let me repeat: after seasoning, the wok should never be scoured. I find that if there is any residual gravy which stubbornly refuses to wash off with ordinary soap and water, a little salt and a paper towel do a fine job. As you use the pan more and more, it will gradually become entirely seasoned and turn from a shiny metallic appearance to a seasoned black.

The most versatile of all utensils in a Chinese kitchen is the *choy doh*, or Chinese kitchen knife. This is the knife that looks like a cleaver and is always seen clutched in the hand of any caricature of a buck-toothed Chinese chef. I suppose to the novice it is quite an imposing piece, for inevitably women are intimidated in the beginning. This is not so, though, as time goes on. Once they have used it and discover how versatile and safe it is, it becomes an indispensable item in their kitchens. I would say of all the utensils, it is the most popular in my course and has won avid converts who swear by it and who have even dispensed with all their other knives.

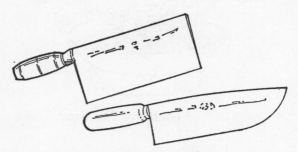

Two types of *choy dohs*

There are two types of choy dohs. The smaller, lighter type is used for slicing both vegetables and meats, and the heavier, larger type is used, as a meat cleaver would be, to chop bones. Not only is the lighter type used for slicing but it can also chop, shred, dice, and peel. Its broad blade is used to transport the prepared food from the chopping block to the pan, and the base of the handle is used to mash ingredients. One needs a whole battery of knives, and a mortar and pestle, to replace the Chinese knife.

The choy dohs are made of carbon steel. This is highly rustable metal so the knives should not be left to drain after washing but dried immediately and put away. Carbon steel is preferred because it is easier to sharpen, taking an edge almost immediately as opposed to stainless steel, which is unsatisfactory because it is a hard metal and very difficult to sharpen.

A piece which adds distinct character to anyone's kitchen is the Chinese *jahm bahn*, or cutting board. This is not an ordinary cutting board for actually it is a cross section of a tree trunk. This piece adds much color to any kitchen but a good hardwood chopping board is easily substituted.

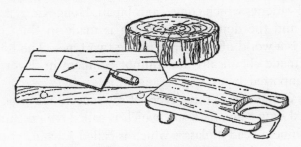

The *jahm bahn*, with substitutes

INGREDIENTS

Soy sauce is the most essential ingredient in Chinese cooking, or for that matter in Japanese or Korean cooking. It has a typical flavor for which there is no substitute. It can be used in all dishes except, of course, in desserts.

There are two types of soy found in this country, the imported varieties which come from Japan, Hong Kong, and Formosa, and the domestic soy which is made in this country. There is a world of difference in the two types. The domestic soy is made chemically and cannot compare in flavor to the aged imported types.

The Chinese have three types of soy sauce. Light soy, which is called *sang chau*, dark soy, which is called *see au*, and thick soy, Chinese bead molasses which is called *jee yau*.

Sang chau is a soy made from extracts of soy bean curd, salt, sugar, and flour. It is a delicate light sauce used as a table sauce for dipping and in dishes where a hint of the flavor of soy is desired but not the color, as in soups.

See au, or dark soy, is made from extracts of soy bean curd, salt, sugar, flour, and caramel. It is fuller bodied, richer, darker in color, and thicker in consistency than light soy sauce. See au is used in all dishes where not only the rich flavor but the dark color of soy are desirable. It is sometimes labeled black soy. Japanese soy sauce falls somewhere between the two Chinese sauces and, if the Chinese types are unavailable, is preferable to domestic soy.

Jee yau is Chinese bead molasses. It is thick and viscous. It is used only in minute amounts to add color to a dish. It should not be used in large quantities where it can be tasted. Jee yau is used in such dishes as beef and peppers or sweet-and-sour spare-ribs, where a dark rich brown gravy is desired. I have found that it works quite well in gravies for American dishes.

Rice wine was always used in China for added flavor in a cooked dish. In America, sherry is the closest substitute for yellow rice wine. I suggest a good sherry, not necessarily the most expensive one but one which you would not hesitate to serve at the table or as an apéritif. It should be on the dry side.

Monosodium glutamate is a white-colored grainy chemical that, used in small quantities, enhances the natural flavor of meats and vegetables. It can be found on the supermarket shelves under such trade names as "Ac'cent" or "Zest." The Chinese call it Mei Jing and the Japanese have a trade name for it, "Aginomoto." Originally it probably was discovered from the soy bean because, when cooked, soy beans yield a product which contains 55 per cent glutamic acid. This was probably converted to monosodium glutamate by drying. The Japanese originally used fermented muscle-of-flour, or flour gluten, which they dried to produce monosodium glutamate. Actually it can be found in any protein wheat flour. This chemical is used in fairly large amounts in restaurants, but for home cooking, if good quality ingredients are used and the food is well prepared, only tiny quantities are necessary. When used excessively, it tends to give all dishes a mechanical sameness in taste.

Concentrated chicken stock is used by the Chinese in place of water for gravies. Chicken stock is preferred to beef stock because it has a more delicate flavor. In any Chinese restaurant, one will always find a large pot simmering which acts as catch-all for chicken parts. This is the master stock pot, and the stock from this pot is used in all gravies and soups. For the busy housewife who cannot make her own stock, I suggest canned chicken broth. The canned broth is more convenient than bouillon cubes as it doesn't require boiling water or adjusting of seasoning. One word of caution: be sure that you don't select one that has other seasoning added besides salt and monosodium glutamate. When using concentrated stock, generally speaking the amount of monosodium glutamate goes down proportionately.

The Chinese use *peanut oil or a vegetable oil* for frying. Hydrogenated or animal fats are not used, as they tend to smoke at the high temperatures required for stir frying. In China, lard was sometimes used when vegetables were being cooked, but that practice has been given up here in America since vegetables cooked in lard cannot be reheated and eaten later.

Cornstarch is used as a binder. It thickens gravies, and a small amount is used on meats, especially coarse meats, to give a smooth texture to the surface of the meat. When you are making several chow dishes (two or three), I suggest having a mixture of half cornstarch and half water (a 1 to 1 formula) by the side of the burner. Add it a tablespoon at a time to thicken gravies. One word of caution: in using cornstarch one must be certain that it cooks for a few minutes in the gravy, since uncooked cornstarch imparts a grainy texture to the dish.

Salt is used in addition to soy, and sometimes exclusively where a "white" gravy is desired. The Chinese add salt to the pan first, after the peanut oil is heated. This helps dissolve the salt and provides for a more evenly seasoned dish.

A little *sugar* is always added at the end of a stir fry dish. The amount varies from ¼ to ½ teaspoon—usually ¼ teaspoon. This is done because it is believed that a small amount of sugar enhances the natural flavors of the food. Sugar is never added in the beginning of the cooking, as it would burn at such high temperatures.

Aside from these basic ingredients, two fresh spices are absolute musts in any Chinese kitchen: garlic and fresh ginger root.

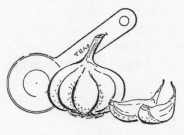

Garlic

Garlic is a bulb that belongs to the onion family and has a strong flavor. It should be purchased fresh by the bulb and each clove should be firm and have a pinkish tinge.

Garlic can be used two ways. When just a hint of the flavor is desired, a clove of garlic is placed in the hot oil and cooked until brown, then removed; or the clove may be impaled on a cooking fork and rubbed around the oiled surfaces of the pan, again while the pan is on a high flame. These methods are used when a vegetable, such as asparagus, is stir fried or for delicate dishes. The second way of using garlic is to mince it finely and use it as one of the ingredients in the dish.

The Chinese peel garlic in a very simple way—by placing it on the chopping board and giving the clove a slight tap with the broad side of the choy doh, or Chinese vegetable-and-meat knife. This separates the covering from the clove, and the exterior can easily be peeled off. If the garlic is to be minced, the next step is to repeat the same action but to bring the choy doh down much more decisively and smash the clove. The broad surface of the knife should be kept absolutely parallel to the chopping board to prevent splattering on the kitchen walls. Then the garlic can be minced finer with the cutting edge of the knife. With a conventional kitchen knife, it would be impossible to use this method.

The French and Italian schools frown on the cook who adds garlic to a pan being heated with a high flame. They believe in cooking garlic very slowly in butter or olive oil. The Chinese have been adding garlic to oil in a pan over a high flame for centuries; the trick here is to know when to add the first ingredient and just how long to cook the garlic without burning it. Garlic is cooked until it stops sizzling; then the first ingredient is added to the pan. This automatically lowers the temperature of the pan. With constant stirring, the garlic will not burn.

In Chinese restaurants, garlic is minced all at once and kept in peanut oil and salt beside the range in an open container. Garlic will keep until used up in this way. If you prepare garlic ahead of time in this manner, keep it refrigerated in a tightly covered jar.

Fresh ginger

When the Chinese refer to *ginger*, they mean the part of the plant that is the tubular root. It is used fresh, either shredded, minced finely, sliced, or smashed. In stir fried dishes it is usually sliced or smashed. Smashing a chunk of ginger, I believe, brings out the full flavor of this spice. When ginger is smashed, a small portion is sliced off the root—size approximately ½ inch by ½ inch—and the broad blade of the choy doh is brought down with a firm tap. The fibers hold the smashed ginger together, and this makes it simple to remove after the dish is cooked. It is usually shredded very finely when used in steamed dishes. It is minced finely when used in chopped dishes. You should try to buy ginger when it is as young as possible. The best time is during the spring. The root is striated horizontally with ridges approximately ¾ inch apart and the skin is smooth. If the root looks dark and the skin shriveled, chances are the ginger has been around for quite a period of time. The inside is a light-yellow fibrous mass. The fibers run vertically down the root and, when ginger is shredded, the shreds are sliced in the same direction as the fibers. If you examine a cross section of a slice of ginger closely, you will see two well-defined sections, a tender portion directly beneath the skin surface and a fibrous center. The portion directly beneath the skin surface is the younger portion of the root and therefore has a subtler, more desirable taste. The center portion is the older part of the root and has a more powerful, less desirable taste. It is my contention that one should not peel ginger root but merely wash it thoroughly and lightly scrape the skin off before use.

Ginger keeps for approximately three weeks in the vegetable compartment of the refrigerator. If it is more convenient, because of distance and difficulty in purchasing it, ginger can be buried in a pot of sand or soil. If the soil is watered frequently, ginger will keep until it is entirely used up.

If you find that fresh ginger is absolutely impossible to purchase, powdered ginger may be used (although it is a very poor substitute). In this case one would use half as much as the recipe calls for.

CHINESE INGREDIENTS

Authentic Chinese cooking cannot possibly be achieved unless the cook has some knowledge of Chinese ingredients —how to identify them and how they are used. More important from an economic point of view, one should know how to store the ingredients and know how long they keep. By ingredients I mean vegetables, dried ingredients, sauces, natural seasonings, dried and powdered herbs and spices, and miscellaneous seasonings. The good Chinese chef has a working knowledge of all these things and achieves variations by combining them cleverly.

During my courses, I was constantly asked by housewives, "How do you keep such and such and how long does it keep?" This is very important, especially in an American kitchen where Chinese cooking would be done at best once a week.

On the following pages is a narrative description of typically Chinese ingredients accompanied when possible by a drawing. A standard measuring teaspoon 3⅜ inches long is included in each drawing to give the reader an idea of the actual size of each ingredient. Along with the description will be instructions on how to store it, how long it keeps, how it is available, and how it is used.

Vegetables

BAMBOO SHOOTS (*jook soon*) Antique-ivory-colored, young bamboo shoots come canned two ways, in water or brine. I have noticed that bamboo shoots packed in water are becoming more and more popular and are stocked by some supermarkets as well as Chinese grocery stores. The type

Bamboo shoot (*jook soon*)

packed in brine is not used in ordinary cooking. Bamboo shoots are used mainly as a filler in dishes. They add texture and are used often by the Chinese because they combine so well with everything. After the can is opened, the water should be drained off, and the remainder of the shoots not used should be transferred to a clean glass jar. Cover them with fresh water and keep the jar tightly covered and refrigerated. If the water is changed every other day, the shoots should last a month.

BEAN SPROUTS (*ngah choy*) These tiny sprouts have pale-yellow heads (often covered with an olive-colored jacket) with

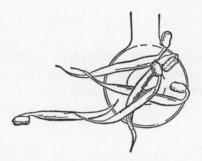

Bean Sprouts (*ngah choy*)

white bodies. The jackets should be removed when washing the sprouts and the tails plucked if one has the patience. The sprout so often referred to as the bean sprout is actually a pea sprout, sold fresh by the pound in Chinese grocery stores and canned (precooked), labeled bean sprouts, in some supermarkets. True bean sprouts are a larger variety. Sprouts combine well with other vegetables and meats and give a crunchy, nutty texture to dishes. Fresh ones should be placed in a container filled with water and refrigerated. The water should be changed daily. The sprouts keep four to five days. Some housewives blanch the sprouts in order to keep them longer, but I feel that much of the texture is lost with this method.

BITTER MELON (*fooh quar*) The bright-green balsam pear is easily identified by its distinct wrinkled surface. It is sold fresh by the pound in Chinese grocery stores. This vegetable

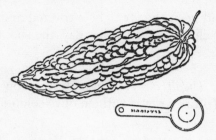

Bitter Melon (*fooh quar*)

is popular during the summer months as it has a bitter but cool flavor. It should be stored in the crisper or in plastic bags in the refrigerator. It will keep from twelve to fourteen days.

CHINESE CABBAGE (*bok choy* or *bok toy*) This vegetable should have pristine white stalks and deep-green leaves when purchased. It is sold in Chinese stores but can be found in some

Chinese Cabbage (*bok choy* or *bok toy*)

supermarkets in Arizona and California. It is mainly cooked in stir fried dishes because of its wonderful crisp texture. It should be stored like Chinese celery cabbage. The younger bok choy, preferred by housewives, is called *choy sum*.

CHINESE CELERY CABBAGE (*siu choy*) This attractive vegetable with white stalks and a leafy light-green fringe is sold by weight in all Chinese grocery stores and in many supermarkets

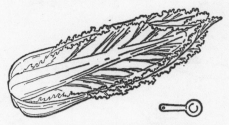

Chinese Celery Cabbage (*siu choy*)

and vegetable stores. It is also called napa. It is prepared in many ways and recently has become a very popular ingredient in good old American tossed salads. Like all fresh leafy vegetables, it should be refrigerated in the crisper or in plastic bags. It keeps for a little over a week but should be used up before it becomes blemished and wilted.

CHINESE BROCCOLI (*guy lon*) This green vegetable, sold in Chinese grocery stores, is a more delicate version of its Ameri-

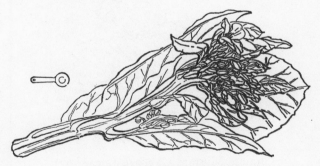

Chinese Broccoli (*guy lon*)

can counterpart. It is superb stir fried alone or with meat and should be stored in the same way as Chinese cabbage.

CHINESE CHIVES (*gow choy*) This cross between a scallion and a chive with long flat green leaves is sold by the bunch in Chinese grocery stores. Like the chive, it does wonders for

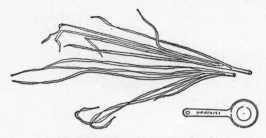

Chinese Chives (*gow choy*)

the simple egg. It is used in stir fried dishes and goes well with noodles. It should be stored bone dry in the crisper or in plastic bags in the refrigerator and used as quickly as possible. It will keep for about a week but begins to give off a very strong odor as it gets old.

CHINESE MUSTARD CABBAGE (*guy choy*) Jade green in color, this cabbage has a marvelous bitter flavor. It is sold by weight

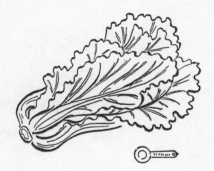

Chinese Mustard Cabbage (*guy choy*)

in Chinese grocery stores and is used in soups or stir fried dishes. It should be stored in the same way all fresh vegetables are kept and should last seven days or so.

PICKLED CABBAGE (*hahm* or *shuen choy*) Sold straight from the pickling barrel or bottled, pickled mustard green is darker green than the fresh mustard green. It is used in stir fried dishes or with noodles. The bottled type may be kept in the pantry until used; the loose type should be used immediately or kept refrigerated for not longer than five days.

SNOW PEAS (*soot dow*) Known also as French peas, sugar peas, or *mange-tout*, this yellowish-green pod is sold fresh by weight in Chinese grocery stores and may be found in some specialty vegetable stores. It is a gourmet's delight and is eaten raw by some. More expensive by weight than steak, this

Snow Peas (*soot dow*)

crisp, delicate vegetable is used mainly in stir fried dishes by the Chinese and in salads by some gourmets. Because of the prohibitive price, the quantities purchased are so small that it is used up almost immediately and rightly so. But if one should have occasion to store snow peas, they should be stored like any other fresh vegetable and used up within a few days.

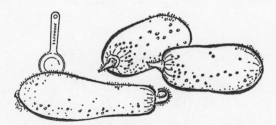

Summer or Hairy Melon (*jeet quar*)

SUMMER OR HAIRY MELON (*jeet quar*) Abundant during the summer, and therefore often referred to as summer melon, this medium-green melon with spines has a delicate flavor reminiscent of squash. Soup made from summer melon is a favorite in the summer among Cantonese. Summer melon also may be braised. It should be stored, like all fresh vegetables, in the refrigerator in plastic bags or in the crisper, and will keep for two weeks or so.

Tea Melons (*cha quar*)

TEA MELON (*cha quar*) Cha quar is sold in cans. It is preserved in honey and comes either combined with ginger or plain. It is cooked any number of ways or eaten as is—cold.

WATER CHESTNUTS (*mar tai*) This popular vegetable is sold fresh by weight or in cans, peeled. The fresh water chestnut is available in Chinese grocery stores; the canned type may be purchased in Chinese grocery stores and some supermar-

Water Chestnuts (*mar tai*)

kets. Peeled water chestnuts should be refrigerated in a tightly covered jar, and the jar should be filled with water which should be changed every other day. The chestnuts should keep from four to six weeks in this way. They lose their texture and crumble as they age. Water chestnuts are like bamboo shoots and go well in any combination.

WATER LILY ROOT (*lien ngow*) This reddish-brown tuberous root of the water lily is used to make soup. It can also be

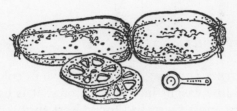

Water Lily Root (*lien ngow*)

braised. If purchased fresh, it keeps for three weeks in the vegetable compartment of the refrigerator. It is available only in Chinese grocery stores.

WINTER MELON (*dung quar*) This impressive melon is the size of a pumpkin. It has a light-green-colored skin which is coated with white, giving the entire melon a frosted look.

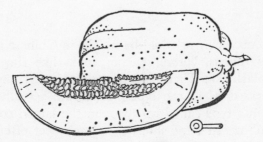

Winter Melon (*dung quar*)

The inside meat is white and makes an elegant soup and can also be braised or red cooked. Sold sectioned by weight in Chinese grocery stores, it should be kept refrigerated in plastic bags or in the crisper, where it will keep three to six days.

With vegetables the reader should keep in mind that conditions vary from area to area and indeed from refrigerator to refrigerator. The times I give are conservative but are based on one important factor—that the vegetable is purchased absolutely fresh.

Dried Ingredients

CHINESE OYSTERS (*ho see*) Amber to brown in color, the dried oyster is sold by weight in Chinese stores. It is used in many ways but first must be soaked for at least thirty-six hours and

Chinese Oysters (*ho see*)

then cleaned. It may be kept in a tightly covered jar in the pantry and like all dried ingredients will keep until used entirely.

CLOUD'S EARS (*wun ye*) Sold by weight in Chinese stores, this cultivated fungus, before soaking, looks like tiny pieces of charred black ash. There is some confusion among amateur Chinese cooks as to the types. There are actually two, the smaller, finer type called *wun ye* and the larger, coarser type called *mok ye*. In some shops the storekeeper often confuses the two. When soaked, the fungus becomes velvety brown in

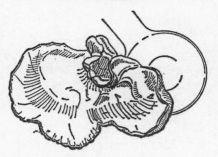

Cloud's Ears (*wun ye*)

color but, when cooked, it actually adds a crisp texture to dishes. In the dried form it can be stored like any other dried goods. After it has been soaked, it may be kept refrigerated in a covered container for six days.

LILY FLOWERS (*gum jum*) Usually prepackaged by weight, the yellow-brown dried-lily flower can be purchased only in Chinese grocery stores. After soaking for approximately fifteen

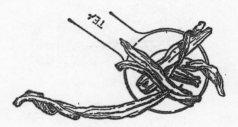

Lily Flowers (*gum jum*)

minutes until soft, gum jum is usually used in long-cooking dishes. It adds a distinct sweetish aromatic flavor to any dish. Lily flowers are stored like any other dried goods.

MUSHROOMS (*dung goo*) Most of our supply of these black dried mushrooms now comes from Japan where they are known as *shiitake*. Dung goo may be purchased in any Chinese or Japanese grocery store. These fragrant mushrooms

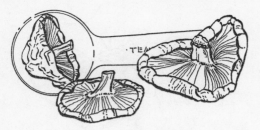

Mushrooms (*dung goo*)

are first soaked until soft and used in literally any dish except dessert. They have an almost meaty texture and superb flavor.

RED DATES (*hoong jo*) These dried dates with shriveled shiny red skins are sold by weight in Chinese grocery stores. They are used to add their particular sweet flavor to long-cooking

Red Dates (*hoong jo*)

dishes, especially soups, desserts, and fish dishes. They should be kept in a tightly covered container in the pantry and will last until used entirely.

SALTED FISH (*hahm yu*) Dried salted fish is sold by the pound in Chinese stores. It is usually served steamed with ginger. It may be kept in the pantry well wrapped, as it has quite a penetrating odor. It will keep until completely used.

SALTED TURNIP (*chung choy*) This prepackaged salted and dried turnip is available in Chinese grocery stores. It comes

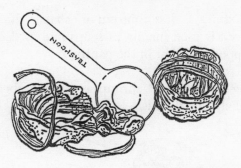

Salted Turnip (*chung choy*)

two ways, in flat sheets or rolled in neat balls. It is used in any dish, but especially in steamed dishes for its salty flavor and chewy texture. It should be stored like all other dried goods.

SCALLOPS (*gong yu gee*) Dried scallops are cylindrical in shape, amber to brown in color, and are sold exclusively in

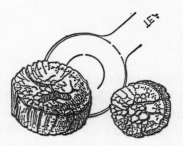

Scallops (*gong yu gee*)

Chinese stores. They are used in many ways, as in *congee* or longer-cooking dishes. Dried scallops should be stored like any other dried goods.

SEAWEED (*gee choy*) Dried seaweed may be purchased in Japanese stores where it is called *nori*. The Japanese variety comes in uniformly thin, purplish sheets; the type available in Chinese stores is less uniform in shape, thickness, and color. Seaweed is used mainly in soups and as decoration. It may be wrapped and kept in the pantry.

SHRIMP (*har mei*) Dried shrimp is deep amber in color, hard, and finely salted. It is sold by weight in any Chinese or

Shrimp (*har mei*)

Japanese grocery store and is used in soups (it makes a wonderful stock) and longer-cooking dishes. Dried shrimp is kept like any other dried goods.

Sauces

BROWN OR YELLOW BEAN SAUCE (*mien see*) This sauce consists of aromatic brown soy beans in a semi-mash. It comes canned and is carried by Chinese grocery stores. The Japanese also have types of bean mash which they call *miso*. Used as a seasoning in dishes, mien see adds a salty, full-bodied flavor. After the can is opened, the sauce should be transferred to a covered jar and kept either in the pantry or the refrigerator. If it is kept in the pantry over six months, however, the sauce tends to change color. If refrigerated, it should last until used entirely.

CHINESE BEAD MOLASSES OR THICK SOY (*jee yau*) Thick soy is canned and carried by Chinese stores. After the can is opened, thick soy should be transferred to glass containers and stored in the pantry. This viscous black sauce is used to make gravies a richer brown color. Caramelized sugar may be substituted.

DUCK SAUCE (*shuen moy jheung*) This plum sauce is reddish amber in color. The imported type is sold only in Chinese grocery stores; the domestic type is bottled and carried by both Chinese stores and some supermarkets. It is used as a condiment on the table to accompany such dishes as roast duck, spare-ribs, egg rolls, and roast pork. It should be refrigerated. Sometimes the sauce is too tart and can easily be made more palatable by adding sugar. It will keep until entirely used.

FERMENTED BEAN CURD (*foo yu*) Often called Chinese cheese, foo yu is bean curd fermented in alcohol and brine (the alcohol being rice wine). It is sold in bottles in Chinese grocery

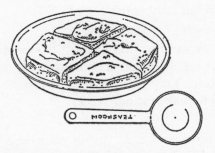

Fermented Bean Curd (*foo yu*)

stores. It is used as a condiment on the table with a little peanut oil and sugar sprinkled over the top, and can also be mixed with cooked vegetables. It is tangy and has the consistency of Camembert cheese. The bottle should be kept in the pantry, and the contents will keep until entirely used.

HOISIN SAUCE (*hoisin jheung*) A rich, dark-auburn sauce made from beans, it sometimes comes with chili added, and is available canned or bottled in Chinese grocery stores. It is used as a condiment on the table or as a seasoning in cooking. After the can is opened, hoisin should be transferred to a covered jar and refrigerated.

OYSTER SAUCE (*ho yau*) This dark-brown essence of oysters is bottled. Both domestic and imported types are carried by Chinese grocery stores; the imported type is superior in flavor. Oyster sauce is used in cooking as a seasoning or may be used at the table for dipping. It should be stored in the pantry in the original container and is good until used completely.

RED BEAN CURD (*nom yu*) Preserved bean curd with red coloring in it, nom yu is available in cans at Chinese grocery stores. It is used as a seasoning in cooking. After the can is opened, the remainder of the bean curd should be transferred to a tightly covered jar and refrigerated. In this way, nom yu should last until entirely used.

SESAME PASTE OR BUTTER (*ma jheung*) Sesame butter is available in cans or bottles under various trade names at any health-food store. Keep refrigerated until entirely used. Ma jheung is used to make various sauces.

SOY SAUCE, LIGHT AND DARK (*sang chau* and *see au*) Soy sauce comes bottled or canned. The domestic type is carried by supermarkets. The imported type may be purchased at any Japanese or Chinese grocery store. It should be kept tightly covered in the original bottle in the pantry. If canned, the soy should be decanted to glass containers which should be sealed and stored in the pantry.

TEN-FLAVORED SAUCE (*subgum jheung*) Identical in color and appearance to hoisin sauce, subgum jheung is actually a spicier and smoother flavored hoisin.

Natural Seasonings

CHINESE PARSLEY (*yeen sai*) This green fresh herb is sold by weight in Chinese grocery stores and it may be purchased

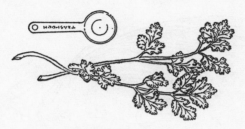

Chinese Parsley (*yeen sai*)

in Spanish stores as *cilantro*. It is fresh coriander. It has a distinct musky flavor and the Chinese use it as a garnish. Yeen sai should be stored bone dry in the crisper or in plastic bags in the refrigerator. It will keep four or five days.

GARLIC (See page 13.)

GINGER (See page 14.)

LEEK (*daai gow choy*) Sold in bunches in Chinese grocery stores or in the vegetable departments of supermarkets, this member of the onion family with yellowish-green flat

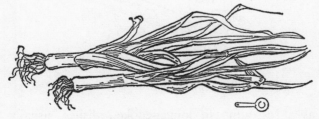

Leeks (*daai gow choy*)

leaves is used in many dishes. It should be refrigerated in the crisper or in plastic bags and will keep for a week.

SCALLIONS (*choong*) In some sections of this country scallions are often referred to as long onions or green onions. They are sold by the bunch in supermarkets and are used mainly

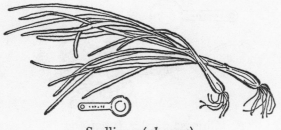

Scallions (*choong*)

as a garnish or seasoning. They should be refrigerated in the crisper or in plastic bags where they will keep for a week or so.

Dried and Powdered Herbs and Spices

ANISE PEPPER OF CHINA (*far jiu*) Far jiu is a deep-scarlet pod with a brown-black seed, which is actually a whole peppercorn. It is sold by weight in any Chinese herb store. It is

Anise Pepper of China (*far jiu*)

used as a seasoning in longer-cooked dishes, usually with star anise. Keep in tightly covered jars in the pantry.

FIVE-FLAVORED SPICE POWDER (*ng heung fun* or *heung new fun*) This spice is a fragrant reddish-brown powder made up of ground Chinese star anise, fennel, anise pepper of China, cloves, and cinnamon. Sold by weight in Chinese grocery stores, it is used as a seasoning and goes especially well in pork, chicken, or duck dishes. It should be stored as one would store any spice.

MONOSODIUM GLUTAMATE (*mei jing*) See text page 11.

STAR ANISE (*bot gok*) This spice, which is burnt sienna in color, is sold only in Chinese grocery stores. It is used

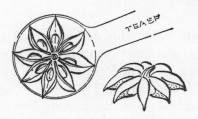

Star Anise (*bot gok*)

mainly in red cooked dishes and with poultry. It should be kept in tightly covered jars in the pantry.

TANGERINE PEEL (*gwo pei*) The dried orange-brown wedge of tangerine skin is sold by weight in Chinese herb stores.

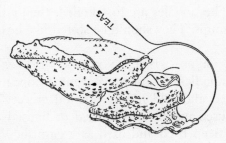

Tangerine Peel (*gwo pei*)

Gwo pei has a powerful flavor and should be used sparingly. It is mainly used in congee, soups, or steamed dishes.

Other Seasonings

BLACK BEANS (*dow see*) These tiny oval black beans are available canned or fresh at Chinese grocery stores. The fresh type is preferable. Used in fairly generous amounts and always with garlic, dow see adds a spicy piquant flavor to any dish. It should be kept in a tightly covered jar in the pantry. Some restaurants saturate the beans in peanut oil and salt to keep them from drying out.

SESAME OIL (*ma yau*) This amber-colored oil made from sesame seeds has a distinct bouquet and superb nutty flavor. It is sold bottled in oriental grocery stores or at any health-food store and is used in small amounts in soups and many other dishes. Sesame oil makes a magnificent salad dressing. It should be kept in the pantry for not longer than a year.

Noodles and Wrappers

BOXED NOODLES (*goon mein*) These dehydrated noodles are much like boxed spaghetti but a bit more rubbery in consistency when cooked. Goon mein is carried by Chinese grocery stores. The noodles are first boiled, then either stir fried or added to soups. They should be stored like boxed spaghetti.

CELLOPHANE OR PEA STARCH NOODLES (*fun see*) Very fine, white, dried noodles, almost translucent in appearance, fun see is prepackaged and sold in any oriental grocery store. These noodles are used mainly in stir fried or braised dishes. They may also be deep fried and used as a garnish. Wrapped and stored in the pantry, fun see will keep indefinitely.

EGG ROLL WRAPPERS (*chuen guen pei*) These fresh squares of pressed dough may be purchased in Chinese grocery stores. They are used to make egg rolls or spring rolls. The wrappers should be refrigerated and will keep for three or four days.

FRESH EGG NOODLES (*dun mein*) Chinese egg noodles are sold by Chinese grocery stores or noodle factories in one-pound packages. They should be boiled "al dente" about six minutes; they are used to make stir fried noodle dishes or soup noodle dishes. The uncooked noodles should be refrigerated, tightly wrapped in plastic bags, and will keep for about three weeks.

RICE STICKS (*mei fun*) These very thin chalk-white noodles resemble cellophane noodles in appearance but are cut in uniform lengths and have an entirely different texture. They should be either preboiled or steamed in perforated containers, and are used to make various dishes. They should be stored in containers in the pantry and will last until entirely used.

WONTON WRAPPERS (*wonton pei*) Fresh 3½-inch squares of pressed dough, which are sold in Chinese grocery stores or noodle factories. They are used to make wonton and various steamed pastries. The fresh wrappers should be kept refrigerated in Saran Wrap and will keep for four or five days. After this they tend to lose their original texture and become stiff and hard to work with.

Miscellaneous Ingredients

ABALONE (*bau yu*) The abalone is a sea mollusk with a spiral shell. It is available at Chinese or Japanese grocery stores either canned or dried. Abalone is used in countless dishes by the Chinese. Some people dislike it because they say it

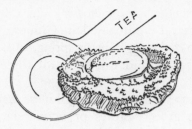

Abalone (*bau yu*)

has the texture of shoe leather but, if prepared correctly, it is very tender. The dried type keeps like all other dried ingredients. The canned type, once opened, will keep for one week or so in the refrigerator.

BEAN CURD (*dow fu*) These white squares of precipitated soybean milk are rich in protein. Among the less fortunate people of the Orient they are the chief source of protein. Bean curd may be purchased in any Chinese or Japanese grocery store.

Bean Curd (*dow fu*)

If one plans to use it in a week, it may be kept in fresh water in the refrigerator. For longer storage, it should be kept in brine in the refrigerator and the brine should be changed every few days. If stored in this way, bean curd should keep for two weeks.

Dow fu pok is bean curd that has been deep fried until golden in color. It is available in Chinese grocery stores. The Japanese call it *aburage* and sell it in their grocery stores

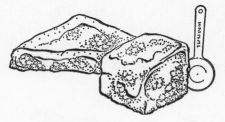

Dow fu pok

also. Dow fu pok should be kept for not longer than three or four days and should be refrigerated.

Fooh jook is the creamy top layer of boiled soy-bean milk. It is dried and comes in stiff long narrow cream-beige strips.

Fooh jook

It is usually used in soups (a good source of protein). Fooh jook may be wrapped and stored in the pantry indefinitely.

Tiem jook is the settled sediment of boiled soy-bean milk. It is dried and comes in stiff, shiny tan-colored sheets that are approximately 5½ inches by 2 inches. Tiem jook is used in stewed meatless dishes. It can be kept wrapped in the pantry indefinitely.

Tiem jook

BELLY PORK (*ng fah yuk*) The cut of meat taken from the loin side of a pig, it is used for bacon in this country. Literally, it is called five-flowered pork because of its alternate layers of fat and lean tissue. To the Chinese the layers

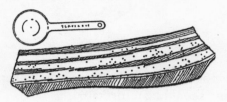

Belly Pork (*ng fah yuk*)

of fat and lean are symbolic of life with its fat and lean years. It should be stored like any other fresh meat.

BIRD'S NEST (*yeen wor*) This dried gelatinous substance, made by a type of swallow to aid in her nest building, is sold packaged at Chinese grocery stores. It is used to make a delicious soup or as stuffing. It should be kept in the pantry and will keep as well as any other dried ingredient.

HUNDRED-YEAR-OLD EGGS (*pei dun*) These chemically aged eggs are covered with a black layer of lime. They are sold by unit at Chinese grocery stores. They should be washed, peeled, sliced, and served as an hors d'oeuvre, or used in congee. The flavor has been described as eggs with a strong overtone of black olives or a firm old cheese. Keep pei dun refrigerated and it should last for several months.

PORK SAUSAGE (*lop chong*) Actually these delicious sausages come stuffed with such various other meats as liver, but pork is the most popular. They are sold by weight in Chinese stores and are used in any number of ways. They may be steamed with rice, then sliced and served as an hors d'oeuvre or as a side dish at the table. They are also used in stir fried

Pork Sausage (*lop chong*)

dishes. Lop chong should be wrapped and refrigerated and will last for several months but tends to dry out as it gets older.

SALTED DUCK'S EGG (*hahm dun*) These eggs are larger than hen's eggs and are soaked in brine. Hahm dun is available at any Chinese grocery store and is sold by the unit. It is served hard cooked as a side dish, or may be used in various steamed dishes. The salted duck's egg should be refrigerated and will keep for about a month.

SHARK'S FIN (*yu chee*) Translucent thread-like dried fins of shark are sold exclusively in Chinese stores. The price may vary anywhere from five to fifty dollars a pound, depending on quality. Shark's fin is used to make a delicious and nutritious soup, as the fin is rich in calcium. I would not suggest an amateur's tackling this dish as it is very difficult to make and only a professional Cantonese chef can prepare it perfectly.

SCHOOLS OF COOKING

AND

METHODS OF PREPARATION

For some time now I have observed that Chinese all share a common trait. Their intense loyalty to the areas of China they originally come from is unsurpassed by anyone else's, even Texans'. China is composed of many provinces, just as the United States is divided into states, and the Chinese are particularly interested in which area one is from. This makes all the difference in the world, for such-and-such a province is, of course, the superior one and all people from this province are superior and the cuisine is without question the greatest that man has created. All people, regardless of what country they are from, have some of this loyalty, but the Chinese have almost developed it into a fine science.

I mention this outstanding trait because the reader must understand it in order to remain unconfused by the differing opinions to be found in current magazine articles and various cookbooks. Americans are just now discovering that Chinese food can mean anything from bland to spicy, from catsup to curry, from hot to cold, and even such exotic-sounding dishes as fried milk. This is so because of the innumerable schools of cooking that exist in China. Many books have been written extolling the superior virtues of the cuisine of the particular province from which the writer happens to come. Even snob appeal has been used to sell one type of cuisine. It is true that each school has its specialty dish, but despite all the claims of superiority and inferiority I find that all the food, regardless of the school of cooking, is prepared in the same manner.

The differences are largely in combinations of spices and sauces. Therefore the purpose of this book is to show you how simple the Chinese method of cooking is if one masters the basic principles. After that it is simply a matter of an imaginative and unprejudiced mind. I have organized the book according to methods of cooking. This I have found to be the clearest and most logical way to teach Chinese cooking. Once the methods are understood, the recipes will be simple.

The recipes I have chosen are from various sections of China, so the Chinese names are in different dialects. The reader should keep in mind that when he enters a Chinese restaurant, he cannot necessarily order every dish that is in this book.

Cantonese restaurants do not serve food from other sections of China, and restaurants that specialize in other than Cantonese cooking serve inferior Cantonese food. A good many of the dishes in this book are not available at all in any restaurant but belong to the category of more or less "home cooked" Chinese dishes.

The Chinese have about a dozen methods of cooking food, each involving different techniques. The best known here in this country is chow, or stir frying. Wet steaming is another method, also called *jing*. *Hoong siu* and *lo soei* are forms of red cooking and involve cooking with soy sauce. *Jow* is deep frying, *mun* is braising, and *shew* is the method used to roast meats. The Chinese also poach, bake, and barbecue. This book intends to cover chow, jing, and red cooking in detail, as they are quite distinct and the only ones peculiar to the Chinese school of cooking. The others that I've mentioned are used in Western cooking and are self-explanatory.

But first things first. Before we begin to cook, the food must be prepared. There are five methods of cutting: slicing, shredding, dicing, chunk, and chopping.

Knife-holding position

In cutting, both hands should participate and synchronize. The knife should be grasped firmly and comfortably. The left hand holds the object to be cut, and the fingernails of the left hand should be tucked in. The second metacarpal, or section of the fingers above the nail, forms a guide surface for the knife. The broad blade protects the fingers as long as the ends of the fingers are kept tucked in. As an added safety measure, the blade or cutting edge of the knife should never be raised above the level of the fingers of the left hand and should be flush against the finger wall. (These principles can also be applied when a conventional kitchen knife is used except that, because the blade is not as wide, there is less leeway.) The left hand also controls the thickness of the slices if moved slowly back as the cutting progresses.

Any knife used should be razor sharp. This is half the battle.

Slicing: In slicing, one should let the knife do the work. Too many people forget this and use undue pressure in slicing vegetables. When working with tomatoes, for example, this can prove disastrous. I'm always able to spot a beginner or novice cook by the way she handles a knife. She works so hard. She puts every ounce of energy behind her cutting.

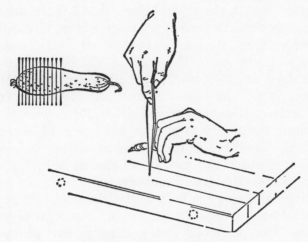

Straight-slicing position

For beginners, slicing should be an easy back and short forward motion, and not a short up-and-down motion with great pressure applied. If the knife is sharp and the motion is easy, the vegetables will cut without undue bruising, mashing, and loss of natural juices. The professional chefs use a quick short up-and-down motion more like chopping, but I suggest that one try my way to begin with.

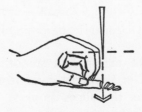

Hand position—straight slicing

There are three ways of slicing: straight slicing, diagonal slicing, and rolling diagonal slicing.

In straight slicing, the knife enters at right angles to the cutting board. The second metacarpals of the left hand, which form a guide as well as protective surface, are absolutely perpendicular with the object being cut. All meats are sliced this way. In order to prevent a stringy texture in meats and to tenderize them, it is important that all meats be straight sliced against the grain. The slices should be approximately an inch long and ⅛ inch thick, the thinner the better. For beginners it will be easier if the meat is slightly frozen. Flank steak is also recommended for the novice because the grain of the meat is so obvious, but one word of caution: flank steak should not be overcooked as it tends to toughen.

Straight slicing is also used on all tender, fleshy vegetables such as bamboo shoots and mushrooms.

In diagonal slicing the knife enters the object on approximately a forty-five-degree slant, cutting a straight object on the bias. The protective and guiding surface of the left hand is now relaxed and also assumes a forty-five-degree

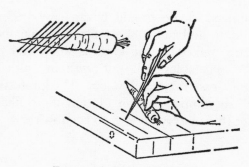

Diagonal-slicing position

angle. In slicing, the action is a smooth backward motion topped off by a roll of the wrist away from the object being sliced. This prevents the slices from sticking together and insures individual pieces.

Hand position—diagonal slicing

Diagonal slicing is used on all stringy, tough, stalky, or cylindrical vegetables. It cuts down cooking time by exposing more surface to heat, insures tenderness, and, in my opinion, is one of the most attractive methods of slicing vegetables. The last method of slicing is the "rolling diagonal" method. This method is used on cylindrical vegetables such as carrots and asparagus. The knife slices diagonally, but the left hand rolls the vegetable toward the cutter after each cut so that the knife cuts through part of the surface made by the last cut. This produces pieces with different shapes and more surfaces which will be exposed to the heat of the pan. It is actually a method of faceting cylindrical vegetables. It makes an interesting product in a dish but I think not as attractive as diagonal slicing.

Shredding: In shredding meats one first straight slices the meats, using the method previously discussed, then cuts the slices into shreds lengthwise approximately ⅛ inch to ¼ inch wide. In shredding fibrous vegetables, such as celery or Chinese celery cabbage, the stalk is straight sliced, with the fibers, into pieces approximately 1 inch to 1½ inches long and ⅛ inch wide. Shredding cylindrical vegetables, such as the cucumber, involves diagonal slicing, where the cucumber is cut on the bias, and then shredding the slices into pieces approximately ¼ inch wide.

When shredding firm vegetables, the tip of the knife is left on the board and only the back end is lifted.

Shredding position with point down

Dicing: Dicing indicates that the pieces must be in squares varying from ⅛ inch to ⅜ inch square. The object is first sliced lengthwise into strips, then the strips are diced.

In preparing irregularly shaped vegetables such as onions, the easiest method is to start from the narrowest section and work toward the bulkiest, then turn the vegetable around and start from the opposite end. This assures control at all times.

Chunk: Chunk is a form of dicing, only the pieces are squares of approximately 1-inch size.

Chopping: In chopping meats the ingredient is first chopped coarsely with the sharp or cutting edge of the knife, then the knife is turned over and the dull part of it finishes the job. Overexuberance in using the sharp edge of the knife may result in having pieces of the chopping board mixed in with the dish.

In chopping vegetables, the blade end of the choy doh is held with the left hand and the blade is lifted only near the handle in a rapid up-and-down motion. The vegetable is brushed into a pile and chopped, and the action is repeated until the process is completed.

Chopping—hand position

I have tried chopping in a blender but have found that it takes experience to know at what point one should stop before the ingredient is puréed. The trick is to start off with small amounts, use high speed, and rapidly flick the switch on and off, checking sizes as you go along.

Although a Chinese chef frowns upon the use of all "new fangled gadgets" I heartily recommend the use of slicers, blenders, meat grinders, and any other modern utensil if it helps make your life easier. Even though the die-hard chef swears that there is a detectable difference in texture (i.e., texture is not as creamy if meat is passed through a grinder), for the busy housewife and mother the difference is negligible considering the time and effort saved.

MASTERING THE METHOD

OF *CHOW*

Chow, or stir frying, is the method of cooking for which the Chinese are best known. This is cooking with high temperatures, using only a small amount of vegetable oil, and constantly stirring the ingredients so that they won't burn. Cooking time is very short, varying from three to six minutes.

Chow was actually the Chinese chef's clever answer to fuel shortage and a simple table service consisting of a pair of chopsticks. It has become the modern chef's answer to the low-cholesterol diet.

In order to achieve perfection with this method of cooking one should understand the techniques and goals which are essential to produce a perfect dish.

Preservation of original color, flavor, texture, and food nutrients is the most important asset of this method. This is achieved by using a high flame at all times and by being absolutely certain the pan is red hot. One should stir constantly after adding the vegetables and meats, in order to prevent burning and thereby preserve the original color of the ingredients. If the ingredients start to burn, the proper thing to do is to add a small amount of oil and stir faster, but at no time should the flame be turned down. The high temperatures bring out the natural flavors and juices of the ingredients and at the same time preserve the original texture of vegetables. Short cooking time is also added insurance that the original texture will be preserved. There is nothing more unpalatable to a Chinese gourmet than over-cooked vegetables. The vegetables should be cooked to the point where they are crisp and their flavor is at its height, although they should not taste raw. This is achieved through experience and training of the eye. Color is an important guide as, generally speaking, all vegetables are done just as they attain the peak of their color. At this point the peak of flavor is also reached. By peak of color I mean the point at which the vegetable is its brightest green: this moment comes just before the color begins to deteriorate to a green-yellow and then to brown or yellow. Along with the deteriorating color, the flavor will also change.

To the cook who is trained in the Western school, vegetables prepared this way will be a revelation and delight, for flavors never before detected will be evident. There is no foolproof method of timing, as it depends upon the age of the vegetables and the intensity of the flame of your particular burner. These are variables and cannot be controlled. The younger the vegetable, the tenderer it is and the less time it will take to cook. The only way is to train oneself to be observant.

The end product of this method should be a dish which presents an artistic picture of symmetry. All components must be uniform in shape: the rule is that usually all imitate the shape of the principal component. An example of this is fried rice in which rice is the principal ingredient and therefore all accessories are diced.

Organization is the key to success when cooking a stir fried dish. In a typical kitchen of a Chinese restaurant, all dry ingredients such as sugar and salt are kept in open containers with teaspoons. Sherry and pepper are kept in containers with perforated tops, and oil is kept in an open container. These are all lined up either beside or above the burners or below on racks. One word sums up the entire set up—accessibility. In a kitchen where stir fried dishes are turned out one after another and made with one wok, speed is of the essence.

If you are planning a really ambitious dinner and have three stir fried dishes on the menu, a similar setup on a smaller scale would be very helpful. Beginners really shouldn't attempt more than one stir fried dish per meal. In this case, I suggest mixing all the ingredients (seasonings and spices) in a measuring cup with cornstarch, water, sugar, monosodium glutamate, soy sauce, and pepper and keeping this mixture beside the pan. The Chinese increase the number of dishes on their menu if more people are expected. One dish suffices for two people and, if they are expecting four people, two dishes, and so forth. But let's face facts— how many of us have time to go through all this elaborate preparation in these days of homes without help? So I suggest that you plan your menus Chinese à la American—that is, plan for fewer dishes and larger quantities.

When working with more than two ingredients, average-size metal trays are a big help. Prepare all the ingredients and arrange them on the tray in piles according to the order they enter the pan.

Be certain that everything is washed, cut, and arranged, and that all spices are mixed before the cooking process starts. Once the cooking starts, it's too late to stop and prepare a forgotten ingredient in the middle of everything. Above all, one should organize a plan of attack before starting. As I sit writing this, I can recall the time one of my students reached the middle of a dish and stopped to look up the "rest of the recipe." Meanwhile the vegetables were furiously cooking away, and by the time she had flipped to the page and read over the recipe they were quite overdone. Or I think of the time a group of students were attempting to make two separate dishes and had their ingredients stacked in neat piles on a tray. They started off very well, but somewhere in the middle of the process of cooking the first dish, which was sweet-and-sour spareribs, they became confused and ended by adding the bean sprouts that were supposed to go into the second dish to their sweet-and-sour spareribs. They gallantly ate their dish, however, claiming that, although it had never been done with bean sprouts, it wasn't such a bad idea. I truly doubt that they liked it so much they repeated it at home.

When stir frying with a wok, certain techniques are used which are not necessary when cooking with a conventional frying pan. As I mentioned before, the siou hok and wok chan should be used. Fill the siou hok, or ladle, with water

Oiling the *wok* with the *siou hok*

and pour this into a measuring cup. This will tell you how much it holds when filled to its maximum capacity. An average-size siou hok holds approximately ½ cup of fluid. From this it is merely another step to judge, when adding liquids, how much ¼ cup is, or one tablespoon. When using a siou hok, measure fluids into it before adding them to the wok. Oil and soup stock are added by using a circular motion around the rim of the pan. In the case of oil, this insures a well-greased pan as the oil dribbles down the sides of the pan and, because of the shape of the wok, covers all surfaces. Salt is always added after the oil, and before any of the actual food, to make for a more evenly seasoned dish.

As the cooking progresses, any other liquid ingredients, such as cornstarch solution or soy sauce, are added by first making a well in the center of the dish and adding the liquid, then stirring. This prevents any one area from absorbing more seasoning than the next and also serves to heat the liquid slightly before mixing it into the dish.

The order in which ingredients are added to the pan is important. Salt, ginger, and garlic are added first after the oil. When one is cooking a number of vegetables, the tougher fibrous vegetables are added next and the tenderer vegetables, such as bean sprouts, lettuce, or tomatoes, last. When cooking a combination of beef and vegetables, the vegetables are cooked first and removed from the pan and the beef is cooked separately approximately three quarters of the way. The vegetables are then put back into the pan and the dish is completed. Cooking the beef last prevents overcooking it and therefore assures tenderness. When working with raw pork, the pork is cooked first, removed from the pan; then the vegetables are cooked and the pork added toward the end. This assures that the pork will be properly cooked.

Seasonings such as sugar and monosodium glutamate are added to approximately ¼ cup cornstarch solution in the siou hok or a measuring cup. A well is made in the food and the mixture is added. When the mixture is heated, the whole dish is stirred and the gravy thickens. The cornstarch not only thickens the gravy but also coats the ingredients and gives the entire dish a glistening appearance.

Above all, patience and practice are important in learning to chow perfectly.

The following recipes were all tested in my kitchen using a twelve-inch wok, so the reader should keep in mind that the recipes are guides and the times are relative. I repeat, color should be your main guide. Start off with a one-vegetable dish by cooking frozen vegetables in the Chinese manner.

Chow Frozen Asparagus

1 box frozen asparagus	1 teaspoon salt
1 clove garlic	¼ teaspoon sugar
2 tablespoons vegetable oil	Dash pepper

PREPARATION: Thaw asparagus. Slice very thin diagonally. Peel clove of garlic.

COOKING: Using a high flame, heat pan and add oil and salt. Rub pan thoroughly with whole clove of peeled garlic until garlic is brown. Discard garlic. Add asparagus and stir for 30 seconds, cover pan for 30 seconds. Uncover, add sugar and dash of pepper, and stir. *Serves 2.*

The asparagus should be between a bright green and dark green along the edges. It should have a crisp but tender texture. Remember that frozen vegetables have high water content so that no additional stock or water is needed to cook them.

This recipe can be used for frozen celery, kale, peas, and spinach.

Chow Frozen Broccoli

1 box frozen broccoli	½ teaspoon monosodium
1 wedge ginger size of quarter	glutamate
2 tablespoons vegetable oil	¼ teaspoon sugar
½ teaspoon salt	Dash pepper

PREPARATION: Thaw broccoli. Cut stems of broccoli diagonally very thin. Cut each floweret into 3 or 4 pieces depending on size. Smash wedge of ginger.

COOKING: Using a high flame, heat pan and add oil and salt. Then add piece of smashed ginger. Add broccoli and stir for

30 seconds. Cover for 4 minutes, stirring occasionally. Uncover, add monosodium, sugar, and pepper. Stir. *Serves 2.*

The broccoli should be bright green, crisp in texture, and at the same time tender.

This recipe can be used for frozen cauliflower, corn, cabbage, and Brussels sprouts.

Chow Frozen Italian Green Beans

1 box frozen Italian beans	½ teaspoon salt
1 wedge ginger size of quarter	¼ teaspoon sugar
2 tablespoons vegetable oil	Dash pepper

PREPARATION: Thaw precut Italian green beans. Smash wedge of ginger.

COOKING: Using a high flame, heat pan and add oil and salt. Add piece of ginger and green beans. Stir for 15 seconds. Cover for 1 minute. Uncover, add sugar and pepper, and stir. *Serves 2 or 3.*

The beans should be bright green and have a crisp, crunchy texture. These beans are not as subtle and sweet in taste as Chinese snow peas but may be used as a substitute if the fresh or frozen snow pea is not available.

This recipe can be used for frozen string beans, mixed vegetables, okra, and Swiss chard.

Ginger and garlic may be interchanged. Generally speaking, one would use ginger for the stronger-tasting vegetables such as the cabbage family.

Now go on to fresh vegetables.

Chow Spinach [CHOW BOR CHOY]

1 *pound spinach*
2 *tablespoons vegetable oil*
½ *teaspoon salt*
1 *clove garlic*

¼ *teaspoon sugar*
¼ *teaspoon monosodium glutamate*
Dash pepper

PREPARATION: Wash spinach and discard stems and bruised areas of leaves. Drain. Peel and mince garlic very fine.

COOKING: Using a high flame, heat pan and add oil and salt. Add garlic and toss in spinach. Cover for 45 seconds. Uncover and stir for 15 seconds. Add sugar, monsodium, and dash of pepper. *Serves 3 or 4.*

The spinach should be dark green and leaves should all glisten. This recipe can be used with any leafy vegetable.

Chow String Beans [CHOW DOW JAI]

½ *pound string beans*
1 *clove garlic*
2 *tablespoons oil*
½ *teaspoon salt*
½ *cup chicken stock or water*

¼ *teaspoon monosodium glutamate*
¼ *teaspoon sugar*
Dash pepper

PREPARATION: Wash beans and string. Break or cut them into 1½-inch lengths. Peel and mince garlic very fine.

COOKING: Using a high flame, heat pan and add oil and salt. Next add garlic. Toss in string beans and stir for 10 seconds. Add stock and cover for 6 to 8 minutes, stirring occasionally. Uncover and add monosodium, sugar, and pepper. Stir. *Serves 2.*

The beans are done when they are bright green, just turning a darker shade of green and are crisp and crunchy in texture.

Two variations of this recipe are achieved by the Chinese in the following ways:

VARIATION I:
After dish is done and flame is off, add 2 bricks Chinese bean curd (foo yu) preserved in brine and rice wine, and stir.

VARIATION II:
1 tablespoon brown or yellow   ½ teaspoon light soy sauce
   bean sauce   ½ teaspoon sugar
½ teaspoon sherry

Mash brown beans and add other ingredients. Stir in just before the flame is turned off.

Chow Young Bok Choy [CHOW CHOY SUM]

1 *pound Chinese cabbage*   ¼ *teaspoon sugar*
1 *wedge ginger size of quarter* ¼ *teaspoon monosodium*
2 *tablespoons oil*   *glutamate*
½ *teaspoon salt*   *Dash pepper*
¼ *cup chicken stock or*
   water

PREPARATION: Wash Chinese cabbage and slice diagonally into slices ½ inch thick. Smash wedge of ginger.

COOKING: Using a high flame, heat pan and add oil and salt. Next add ginger. When pan is red hot, add Chinese cabbage and stir for 45 seconds. Add stock and cover for 1½ minutes. Uncover and stir for 15 seconds. Add sugar, monosodium, and pepper. Stir. *Serves 3.*

Choy sum is the younger, tenderer *bok choy* preferred by Chinese housewives. The restaurants use bok choy because it is less expensive. In home cooking we always include the tops, but in restaurants the tops are omitted and used in soups like wonton soup, because at such high temperatures they wilt.

Chow Carrots [CHOW HOONG LO BAK]

4 carrots	½ teaspoon sugar
1 wedge ginger size of quarter	¼ teaspoon monosodium
2 tablespoons vegetable oil	glutamate
½ teaspoon salt	Dash pepper
½ cup chicken stock or	
water	

PREPARATION: Wash and peel carrots. Slice diagonally approximately 1/16 to ⅛ inch thick. Smash wedge of ginger.

COOKING: Using a high flame, heat pan and add oil, salt, and ginger. Next add carrots and stir. Add stock and cover for 6 minutes. Uncover and stir for 20 seconds and add sugar, monosodium, and pepper. Stir. *Serves 2.*

This recipe is strictly my invention. Try this with cabbage. For a variation make it sweet and sour by adding 2 teaspoons of vinegar and ½ teaspoon of sugar before the flame is turned off.

Some people like their gravies thickened with cornstarch in vegetable dishes. I dislike this and think it unnecessary in the simpler dishes.

Now try combinations of two or more vegetables.

Chow Bean Sprouts and Peppers [CHOW ARE CHOY LOT TZU]

3 cups green peppers
2 hot chili peppers
¾ pound bean sprouts
Thin slice ginger
2 tablespoons vegetable oil
1 teaspoon salt

¼ cup chicken stock or water
1 teaspoon sherry
½ teaspoon monosodium glutamate
¼ teaspoon sugar

PREPARATION: Wash and seed both types of peppers. Slice very thin. Wash bean sprouts and remove tails if you have the patience. Smash ginger.

COOKING: Using a high flame, heat pan and add oil, salt, and ginger. Add peppers and stir for 1 minute. Add bean sprouts and stir. Add stock and cover for 3 minutes. Uncover, add sherry, monosodium, and sugar. Stir. *Serves 3 or 4.*

Green peppers should not be overcooked, as they tend to taste bitter. Again the color should be your main guide in cooking them. They should be a bright green. In this dish, if preferred, the red peppers may be omitted.

Chinese Mixed Vegetables [TZU SAT JING]

1 strand dried bean curd
1 tablespoon lily flowers
8 cloud's ears
4 Chinese mushrooms
12 snow peas
1 cup bamboo shoots
5 water chestnuts
¼ cup carrots
1 wedge ginger size of quarter
2 teaspoons cornstarch with 2 teaspoons water
½ teaspoon sugar

¼ teaspoon monosodium glutamate
Dash pepper
2 tablespoons vegetable oil
1 teaspoon salt
1 cup Chinese cabbage
¼ cup canned or fresh mushrooms
½ cup chicken stock or water
1 teaspoon sherry

PREPARATION: Break dried bean curd into 2-inch lengths and boil for 30 minutes or until soft, or soak overnight in water and, when soft, cut into 2-inch lengths. Soak lily flowers in cold water for 15 minutes along with cloud's ears. Soak mushrooms until softened in cold water, approximately 20 minutes. Shred mushrooms. String snow peas, and if pods are extra large cut in two, using a diagonal cut. Shred bamboo shoots and slice water chestnuts very finely. Slice carrots diagonally and parboil for 1 minute. Wash and smash ginger. Mix cornstarch solution, sugar, monosodium, and pepper and set cup beside pan.

COOKING: Using a high flame, heat pan and add 1 tablespoon of oil and ½ teaspoon of salt. When pan is red hot, add bamboo shoots and chow for 20 seconds. Remove and set aside. Next heat pan again and add 1 tablespoon of oil, ½ teaspoon of salt, and wedge of ginger. Add cabbage and stir. Next throw in two kinds of mushrooms, lily flowers, water chestnuts, bean curd, carrots, cloud's ears, and bamboo shoots. Chow for 15 seconds. Add stock and cover for 1 minute. Uncover, stir, and add snow peas, sherry, and thicken with cornstarch mixture. Stir for 1 minute or until cornstarch has cooked. *Serves 2 or 3.*

This dish is actually a short-cooking modified version of a famous Chinese vegetarian dish often eaten by Buddhist monks. It is known as *lo hon ji* in Canton but one ingredient that is in the original dish is left out and that is *fat choy*, a seaweed resembling hair. I like this Shanghai version because I personally do not like the flavor of fat choy.

This is a delicious as well as elegant vegetable dish to serve and is well worth all the preparation. One hint: cloud's ears and dried bean curd may be made in quantity and kept refrigerated in tightly covered containers and used in other dishes, if used within a week or so.

Now go on to beef-and-vegetable combinations, keeping in mind the fact that beef gets very tough and stringy when overcooked. To prevent this, never add stock to beef as this tends to toughen it. Beef is always cooked last to prevent overcooking it. You may use flank steak, chuck steak, chuck roast, or sirloin.

Beef with Snow Peas [SOOT DOW NGOW]

½ pound beef
½ pound snow peas
2 teaspoons cornstarch mixed
  with 2 teaspoons water
Dash pepper
½ teaspoon sugar
¼ teaspoon monosodium
  glutamate
1 wedge ginger size of quarter
2 tablespoons vegetable oil

½ teaspoon salt
½ cup chicken stock or
  water

Marinade for beef:
1 teaspoon cornstarch
1 teaspoon light soy sauce
2 teaspoons sherry
¼ teaspoon sugar
¼ teaspoon vegetable oil

PREPARATION: Slice beef and add marinade. String snow peas. Mix cornstarch and water and add pepper, sugar, and monosodium. Set beside pan. Smash ginger.

COOKING: Using a high flame, heat pan and add 1 tablespoon of oil, salt, and ginger. Add snow peas, stir, and add stock. Cover for 15 seconds. Uncover, stir, remove, and set aside. Reheat pan and add remaining tablespoon of oil. When pan is red hot, add beef and press against sides of pan. Stir for 45 seconds until beef is three-quarters cooked, then add snow peas and cornstarch mixture. Cook until gravy thickens. *Serves 2 or 3.*

The Chinese housewife always prepares her meats in the marinade mentioned above. The cornstarch coats the meat and prevents loss of juices and at the same time gives the surface of the meat a smooth texture. The other ingredients point up the flavor of the meat. The one drawback in cooking meat that has been prepared in this way is that if the pan is not red hot, the meat slices will stick to it.

Beef with Broccoli [GUY LON NGOW]

½ pound beef
4 cups fresh broccoli
(1 pound)
1 wedge ginger size of quarter
2 teaspoons cornstarch mixed
with 2 teaspoons water
½ teaspoon monosodium
glutamate
Dash pepper
2 tablespoons vegetable oil

½ teaspoon salt
¾ cup chicken stock or
water

Marinade for beef:
1 teaspoon cornstarch
1 teaspoon light soy sauce
2 teaspoons sherry
¼ teaspoon sugar
¼ teaspoon vegetable oil

PREPARATION: Slice beef and add marinade. Wash broccoli and peel off tough outer layer. Slice broccoli stems diagonally into paper-thin slices and divide flowerets into 3 or 4 small sections, depending on size. Smash wedge of ginger. Mix cornstarch, water, monosodium, and pepper. Set beside pan.

COOKING: Using a high flame, heat pan and add 1 tablespoon of oil, salt, and ginger. Add broccoli and stir. Add stock and cover for 6 minutes, stirring occasionally. Uncover, stir, remove, and set aside. Heat pan again and add remaining tablespoon of oil. When pan is red hot, add beef and flatten against sides of pan. Chow for 45 seconds until beef is three-quarters cooked. Add broccoli and stir in cornstarch mixture. Cook until gravy thickens. *Serves 2 or 3.*

Broccoli, like any member of the cabbage family, should not be overcooked otherwise it will taste sulfurous. Color should be the main guide. It is done when it is bright green.

This recipe can be used as a guide to cook beef with cabbage, cauliflower, kohlrabi, kale, Chinese cabbage, Chinese celery cabbage, or any number of other vegetables. The reader should keep in mind that cooking times will vary and should use color as his main guide. Depending on personal taste, one may add 2 teaspoons of soy and cut down some of the salt if one wants a variation.

Beef with Green Peppers, Tomatoes, and Onions [FON CARE LOT TZU NGOW]

½ pound beef
2 large tomatoes
2 green peppers
1 large Spanish onion
1 tablespoon black beans
1 clove garlic
1 wedge ginger size of quarter
2 teaspoons cornstarch mixed
 with 2 teaspoons water
Dash pepper
1 tablespoon dark soy sauce
¼ teaspoon sugar
½ teaspoon monosodium
 glutamate

2 tablespoons vegetable oil
½ teaspoon salt
¾ cup chicken stock or
 water

Marinade for beef:
1 teaspoon cornstarch
1 teaspoon light soy sauce
2 teaspoons sherry
¼ teaspoon sugar
¼ teaspoon vegetable oil

PREPARATION: Slice beef and add marinade. Cut tomatoes into wedges. Seed peppers and slice lengthwise in two, then cut halves into 1-inch squares. Cut onion in wedges approximately same size as peppers. Rinse black beans and mince. Smash garlic and mince. Set aside with black beans. Smash wedge of ginger. Mix cornstarch solution and add pepper, soy, sugar, monosodium, and set beside pan. Parboil peppers for 1 minute (optional).

COOKING: Using a high flame, heat pan and add 1 tablespoon of oil, salt, garlic, and black beans. Next add green peppers and onion and stir. Add stock and cover for 2 minutes. Uncover, stir, remove, and set aside. Reheat pan and add remaining oil and ginger. When pan is red hot, add beef and flatten against sides of pan. Chow for 45 seconds or until beef is three-quarters done. Add green peppers and onion, and when stock boils stir in cornstarch mixture and tomato wedges. Stir until gravy thickens. *Serves 2.*

For the American variation of this dish, leave out the black beans and ginger and increase the sugar to 1 teaspoon.

Shredded Beef with Celery [KAN CHOY NGOW YUK TSE]

½ pound beef
5 stalks celery
1 clove garlic
1 teaspoon cornstarch mixed
  with 1 teaspoon water
¼ teaspoon sugar
½ teaspoon monosodium
  glutamate
Dash pepper
3 tablespoons vegetable oil

¼ cup chicken stock or
  water

Marinade for beef:
1 teaspoon cornstarch
1 teaspoon light soy sauce
2 teaspoons sherry
¼ teaspoon sugar
¼ teaspoon vegetable oil

PREPARATION: Shred beef and add marinade. Slice celery diagonally paper thin or shred celery by cutting into lengthwise strips of 1½ inches. Peel garlic. Mix cornstarch solution and add sugar, monosodium, and pepper. Set beside pan.

COOKING: Using a high flame, heat pan and add 2 tablespoons of oil and rub pan with clove of garlic until garlic is brown. Discard. Add celery, stir, and add stock. Cover and cook for 2 minutes. Stir, remove, and set aside. Reheat pan and add remaining oil. When pan is red hot, add beef and flatten against sides of pan. Chow for 45 seconds until shreds are three-quarters done. Add celery and cornstarch mixture. Stir until gravy thickens. *Serves 2.*

This is a delicious as well as an economical dish. The celery should not be cooked past the point where it loses its crisp, crunchy texture. For a variation try adding sliced water chestnuts and onions.

Shredded Beef with Tea Melon and Ginger [CHA QUAR NGOW YUK TSE]

½ pound beef
½ cup preserved tea melon
  with ginger
2 tablespoons vegetable oil
½ teaspoon salt

Marinade for beef:
1 teaspoon cornstarch
2 teaspoons sherry
¼ teaspoon light soy sauce
¼ teaspoon sugar

PREPARATION: Shred beef and add marinade. Shred tea melon and ginger.

COOKING: Using a high flame, heat pan and add oil and salt. Add beef and stir for 30 seconds. Next add tea melon and ginger. Stir for 1½ minutes. *Serves 2.*

This is an unusual-tasting dish and is one of my favorites.

Ground Beef with Frozen Mixed Vegetables

½ pound ground beef
1 package frozen mixed
  vegetables
1 wedge ginger size of quarter
2 teaspoons cornstarch mixed
  with 2 teaspoons water
½ teaspoon monosodium
  glutamate
¼ teaspoon sugar
1 teaspoon dark soy sauce
Dash pepper

2 tablespoons vegetable oil
½ teaspoon salt
½ cup chicken stock or
  water

Marinade for beef:
1 teaspoon light soy sauce
2 teaspoons sherry
1 teaspoon cornstarch
¼ teaspoon sugar
¼ teaspoon vegetable oil

PREPARATION: Mix marinade into ground beef. Thaw frozen vegetables. Smash wedge of ginger. Mix cornstarch solution and add monosodium, sugar, soy, and pepper. Set beside pan.

COOKING: Using a high flame, heat pan and add oil, salt, and ginger. Add thawed mixed vegetables and stir for 25 seconds. Cover for 1½ minutes. Next add beef and stir, adding chicken stock, for 2 minutes or until beef is nearly cooked. Stir in cornstarch mixture and turn flame off when cornstarch thickens gravy. *Serves 2.*

This is strictly an American dish cooked the Chinese way, but for the novice Chinese cook, it is a good start. I find that my toddler loves it.

Ground Beef with Chinese Vegetables and Cellophane Noodles [NGOW YUK SOONG]

½ pound ground beef
4 large Chinese mushrooms
8 water chestnuts
1 cup Chinese cabbage
¼ cup bamboo shoots
10 snow peas
1 wedge ginger size of quarter
1 clove garlic
2 teaspoons cornstarch mixed with 2 teaspoons water
¼ teaspoon sugar
½ teaspoon monosodium glutamate
Dash pepper
2 cups vegetable oil
1 ounce Chinese cellophane noodles

2 tablespoons vegetable oil
1 teaspoon salt
½ cup chicken stock or water
¼ cup peas
1 tablespoon chopped toasted almonds

Marinade for beef:
1 teaspoon cornstarch
1 teaspoon light soy sauce
2 teaspoons sherry
¼ teaspoon sugar
¼ teaspoon vegetable oil

PREPARATION: Mix marinade into ground beef. Soak Chinese dried mushrooms in cold water for 15 minutes or until soft. Dice mushrooms, water chestnuts, Chinese cabbage, and bamboo shoots. String snow peas and if especially large, slice in half with a diagonal cut. Smash ginger wedge and mince garlic. Mix cornstarch solution and add sugar, monosodium, and pepper. Set beside pan.

COOKING: Heat 2 cups of oil or enough oil to cover one ounce of loosened cellophane noodles. If using an electric deep fat fryer, temperature should be set at 375 degrees. Deep fat fry noodles for approximately 20 seconds on each side. They will puff up almost instantly. Set aside on paper towel. Using a high flame, heat 1 tablespoon of oil, ½ teaspoon of salt, and ginger. Next add Chinese cabbage, bamboo shoots, mushrooms, and chicken stock. Add water chestnuts and peas. Chow for another minute. Remove and set aside. Reheat pan and add 1 tablespoon of oil, ½ teaspoon of salt, and garlic. When pan is red hot, add beef and stir for 1½ minutes until nearly done. Add snow peas and other vegetables, and when gravy boils add cornstarch mixture. Stir until gravy thickens. Remove to serving dish, sprinkle with almonds, and place noodles on top of dish. *Serves 2.*

This is a spectacular dish to serve to company that you want to impress. I usually use a silver server. *Fun see,* or Chinese cellophane noodles, is often deep fried and used as a garnish by the Chinese. It is usually used in this way in chopped meat with vegetables or in shredded meat with vegetables. When deep fried, it resembles the cut waxed paper florists use to pack flowers in. It has no particular flavor but adds a wonderful crisp texture to the dish and, of course, is nice to look at.

Ground Beef with Bean Curd [DOW FU NGOW YUK]

½ pound ground beef
2 bricks bean curd
2 stalks scallions
2 cloves garlic
1 tablespoon cornstarch mixed
with 1 tablespoon water
1 teaspoon dark soy sauce
¼ teaspoon sugar
Dash pepper
2 tablespoons vegetable oil

½ teaspoon salt
½ cup chicken stock or
water

Marinade for beef:
1 teaspoon cornstarch
1 teaspoon light soy sauce
2 teaspoons sherry
¼ teaspoon sugar
¼ teaspoon vegetable oil

PREPARATION: Mix marinade into ground beef. Cut each bean
curd into 9 squares. Mince scallions. Mince garlic very fine.
Mix cornstarch solution and add soy, sugar, and pepper. Set
beside pan.

COOKING: Using a high flame, heat pan and add oil, salt, and
garlic. Next add beef and stir. Add stock and cook for 1 minute. Add bean curd and cornstarch solution. Stir until gravy
thickens. Add scallions. *Serves 2.*

For a variation of this dish, try sprinkling 1 teaspoon of
Szechuan hot oil after the dish is done. This adds extra zest.

Here is a recipe for the hot oil.

Szechuan Oil

1 cup sesame or peanut oil
⅛ ounce coarsely ground red pepper

Heat oil in pan and add pepper. When oil turns red, turn off
flame. Strain into container after it cools. Keep in pantry.

Fried Bean Curd [JEEN DOW FU]

4 bricks bean curd
2 stalks scallions
½ teaspoon salt
2 tablespoons vegetable oil

2 tablespoons dark soy sauce
1 teaspoon sugar
Dash pepper

PREPARATION: Cut each bean curd into 9 squares. Mince scallions.

COOKING: Using a high flame, heat pan and add salt and oil. Fry bean curd until brown. Add other ingredients. *Serves 2.*
For a variation of this dish, try oyster sauce instead of soy sauce.

Kiangsu Egg Dish [MOU SOO YUK]

4 eggs
1 tablespoon water
¾ teaspoon salt
6 lily flowers
10 cloud's ears
1 stalk scallions
½ cup head cabbage
2 ounces fresh pork
1 cup bamboo shoots

2 teaspoons light soy sauce
¼ teaspoon sugar
½ teaspoon monosodium
    glutamate
Dash pepper
2 tablespoons vegetable oil
1 wedge ginger size of quarter
1 teaspoon sherry

PREPARATION: Beat eggs slightly and add water and ¼ teaspoon salt. Soak dried lily flowers in water for 15 minutes or until soft. Soak cloud's ears in water until soft. Cut tops of scallion in 2 inch lengths and shred bottoms. Shred cabbage, pork, and bamboo shoots. Mix soy, sugar, monosodium, and pepper together. Set beside pan.

COOKING: Scramble eggs and set aside. Using a high flame, heat pan and add oil, ½ teaspoon of salt, and ginger. Add

pork and bamboo shoots. Stir fry for 30 seconds. Add sherry.
Next add cabbage, cloud's ears, lily flowers, and cover for 1
minute. Add soy mixture, scallions, and eggs. *Serves 2.*

The French chef would die watching a Chinese chef prepare an omelette. The Chinese omelette is cooked with a high
flame as opposed to the French, which is cooked with a
medium-low flame. The ideal Chinese omelette is brown and
tough on the outside and soft and runny on the inside. This
is because some Chinese omelettes often have as much of the
other ingredients in them as they do egg and the high heat
helps to bind the whole dish. Although the French omelette
is very delicate, there is much to be said about the way Chinese prepare eggs: try a dish and draw your own conclusions.

Chinese Chive Omelette [CHOW DUN]

¼ *pound pork or ham*
1 *cup Chinese chives*
4 *eggs*
1 *teaspoon sherry*
½ *teaspoon monosodium*
  glutamate
1 *teaspoon salt*
¼ *teaspoon sugar*
2 *tablespoons vegetable oil*

Dash pepper

Marinade for meat:
½ *teaspoon cornstarch*
½ *teaspoon light soy sauce*
1 *teaspoon sherry*
Pinch sugar
Few drops vegetable oil

PREPARATION: Shred pork and add marinade. Wash chives
and cut into 3 inch lengths. Beat eggs and add sherry, monosodium, ½ teaspoon of salt, and sugar.

COOKING: Using a high flame, heat pan and 1 tablespoon of
oil and ½ teaspoon of salt. Add pork and stir for 1½ minutes, or until done, and add pepper. Remove from pan and

mix pork and chives into eggs. Reheat pan and add another tablespoon of oil. Here you can either divide mixture in half and make two omelettes or pour all of mixture into pan. As eggs cook, tilt pan so uncooked part rolls under and around cooked part of omelette. Cook for 1½ minutes on each side or until brown. *Serves 2.*

The Chinese chives do to the omelette what chives do for a French omelette—they point up the flavor of the egg.

A note on turning omelettes from two of my outstanding students (both men, of course). One used two dinner plates, sliding the omelette out of the wok onto one plate. Then covering that plate with the other, he flipped the omelette and slid it back into the pan. The other flipped the omelette as one would flip a flapjack. Both methods produced beautiful omelettes which were intact.

Scrambled Eggs with Crab Meat [HAI CHOW DUN]

4 eggs	*Dash pepper*
1 teaspoon salt	*1 stalk scallion*
2 teaspoons sherry	*¼ teaspoon minced ginger*
¼ teaspoon sugar	*½ pound crabmeat*
½ teaspoon monosodium glutamate	*2 tablespoons vegetable oil*

PREPARATION: Beat eggs and add ½ teaspoon of salt, sherry, sugar, monosodium, and pepper. Mince scallion. Mince ginger very fine. If frozen crabmeat is used, thaw completely and discard excess moisture.

COOKING: Using a high flame, heat pan and add oil, ½ teaspoon of salt, ginger and crabmeat. If crabmeat is raw, cook for 45 seconds until done. If cooked, stir and immediately add eggs and scallion. Scramble until firm. *Serves 2.*

Cantonese Egg Foo Young [KWANGTUNG YUNG DUN]

3 eggs
½ teaspoon monosodium
glutamate
1 teaspoon salt
¼ teaspoon sugar
1 teaspoon sherry

4 Chinese mushrooms
1 stalk Chinese cabbage
2 ounces roast pork
3 water chestnuts
2 tablespoons vegetable oil
1 tablespoon bamboo shoots

PREPARATION: Beat eggs and add monosodium, ½ teaspoon of salt, sugar, and sherry. Soak mushrooms in cold water for 15 minutes or until soft. Shred mushrooms, Chinese cabbage, and roast pork. Slice water chestnuts very thin.

COOKING: Using a high flame, heat pan and add one tablespoon of oil and ½ teaspoon of salt. Next add Chinese cabbage, bamboo shoots, mushrooms, water chestnuts, and pork. Stir for 30 seconds and cover for 45 seconds. Mix into lightly beaten eggs. Reheat pan and add 1 tablespoon of oil and pour mixture in. Repeat exact procedure as described in Chinese chive omelette recipe. *Serves 2.*

Egg foo young is basically a leftover dish and almost anything may be used—chicken or shrimp, for example. This is actually how the variations are achieved in restaurants. Just be sure that the ingredients are shredded in order to bind the omelette. Cantonese egg foo young is more or less the deluxe version because of the number of ingredients that go into making it.

Pork is the favorite meat of Chinese housewives, and there are innumerable ways of cooking it. The times are only a guide in the following recipes; just keep in mind that pork is cooked when it turns white. In all these recipes, when I say pork I mean either fresh butt, tenderloin, boned shoulder, or boned chops.

Pork with Oyster Sauce [HO YAU GEE YUK]

½ pound pork
1 wedge ginger size of quarter
2 teaspoons cornstarch mixed
    with 2 teaspoons water
¼ teaspoon sugar
½ teaspoon monosodium
    glutamate
Dash pepper
2 tablespoons oyster sauce
    (or to taste)

2 tablespoons vegetable oil
½ cup chicken stock or water

Marinade for pork:
1 teaspoon cornstarch
2 teaspoons sherry
¼ teaspoon sugar
¼ teaspoon peanut oil

PREPARATION: Slice pork and add marinade. Smash ginger. Mix cornstarch solution and add sugar, monosodium, pepper, and oyster sauce. Set beside pan.

COOKING: Using a high flame, heat pan and add oil and ginger. Next add pork and stir for 3 minutes or until nearly done. Add stock and bring to boil, then add cornstarch mixture and cook until cornstarch thickens. *Serves 2.*
You may substitute dark soy for the oyster sauce.

Curried Pork [GAR LAY GEE YUK]

½ pound pork
¼ cup sliced onion
2 teaspoons cornstarch mixed
    with 2 teaspoons water
½ teaspoon salt
½ teaspoon monosodium
    glutamate

½ teaspoon sugar
Pinch five-flavored spice
    powder (optional)
Dash pepper
4 tablespoons curry powder
½ cup chicken stock or
    water

PREPARATION: Slice pork and onions. Mix cornstarch solution and add salt, monosodium, sugar, five-flavored spice powder, and pepper. Set beside pan.

COOKING: Using a low flame, heat curry in a *dry* frying pan with onion, constantly stirring until the odor of curry becomes very pungent in the kitchen, approximately 3 minutes. Next add pork and stir for 3 minutes. Add stock, at the same time turning flame to high. When stock boils, stir for 5 minutes. Then add cornstarch mixture and cook for 3 minutes. *Serves* 2.

Curry is always pan fried in a dry frying pan, using a low flame. This is a special secret Chinese chefs use because they believe (and I agree) that it really brings out the true flavor of curry. The trick is to stir constantly to prevent the curry from burning.

Now go on to pork with a vegetable. The rule here is to cook raw pork first to insure its being well done.

Pork with Bitter Melon [FOOH QUAR GEE YUK]

½ *pound pork*
2 *pounds bitter melon*
2 *or* 3 *cloves garlic*
1½ *tablespoons black beans*
2 *teaspoons cornstarch mixed
    with* 2 *teaspoons water*
1 *teaspoon light soy sauce*
½ *teaspoon sugar*
½ *teaspoon monosodium
    glutamate*
Dash pepper

2 *tablespoons vegetable oil*
¾ *cup chicken stock or
    water*

Marinade for pork:
1 *teaspoon cornstarch*
1 *teaspoon light soy sauce*
2 *teaspoons sherry*
¼ *teaspoon sugar*
¼ *teaspoon vegetable oil*

PREPARATION: Slice pork and add marinade. Wash bitter melon, cut in half, and dispose of seeds. Slice in 1/16-inch slices. Parboil for 3½ minutes. Drain and rinse. Mince garlic. Rinse black beans and mince. Mix cornstarch solution and add soy, sugar, monosodium, and pepper. Set beside pan.

COOKING: Using a high flame, heat pan and add oil and garlic and black beans. After 30 seconds add pork and stir 3 minutes or until nearly done. Next add bitter melon, stir, and pour in chicken stock. Cover for 2 minutes. Add cornstarch solution and stir until cornstarch thickens. *Serves 2.*

This can be a marvelous dish in the summer: bitter melon leaves a pleasantly cool taste in the mouth. The preboiling of the bitter melon is very important. If it is not boiled to just the right point the dish will be so bitter it will be almost inedible.

Pork with Mushrooms [MOU GOO GEE YUK]

½ pound pork
1 cup mushrooms
1 wedge ginger size of quarter
2 teaspoons cornstarch mixed
   with 2 teaspoons water
¼ teaspoon sugar
1 teaspoon dark soy sauce
½ teaspoon monosodium
   glutamate
2 tablespoons vegetable oil

½ teaspoon salt
¾ cup chicken stock or
   water

Marinade for pork:
1 teaspoon cornstarch
1 teaspoon light soy sauce
2 teaspoons sherry
¼ teaspoon sugar
¼ teaspoon vegetable oil

PREPARATION: Slice pork and add marinade. Wash and slice mushrooms or use canned sliced mushrooms. Smash wedge of ginger. Mix cornstarch solution and add sugar, soy, and monosodium. Set beside pan.

COOKING: Using a high flame, heat pan and add oil, salt, and ginger. Add pork and stir for 3 minutes or until nearly done. Then add mushrooms and stock. Cover for 2 minutes and thicken with cornstarch solution. *Serves 2.*

This recipe can be used as a guide for cooking pork with broccoli, onions, asparagus, or Chinese celery cabbage. Just remember that the times would differ; use color as your main guide.

Pork Chops with Lettuce, Tomatoes, and Onions

3 tablespoons vegetable oil
1½ teaspoons salt
3 1-inch-thick pork chops
2 teaspoons sherry
1 beefsteak tomato
½ heart of celery
½ cup onion
1 cup lettuce
¼ cup catsup
1 tablespoon Worcestershire
  sauce

1 teaspoon sugar
½ teaspoon monosodium
  glutamate
Dash pepper
2 teaspoons cornstarch mixed
  with 2 teaspoons water
½ cup chicken stock or
  water

PREPARATION: Using a high flame, heat pan and add 1 tablespoon of oil and ½ teaspoon of salt. Fry pork chops until
done, and just before turning flame off, sprinkle with sherry.
Let cool, then bone and cut into 1-inch squares. Cut beefsteak
tomato into 8 wedges. Slice celery, onion, and lettuce. Mix
catsup, Worcestershire sauce, sugar, monosodium, and pepper
with cornstarch solution and set beside pan.

COOKING: Using a high flame, heat pan and add remaining
oil and 1 teaspoon of salt. Add celery, onion, and stock, and
cover for 2 minutes. Add meat and lettuce and tomato (in
same order) and stir for 1 minute. Add cornstarch mixture
and cook until it thickens. *Serves 3.*

This is a colorful as well as a delicious dish that's sure to be
a favorite with your family. It is important that one always
cools meat before cutting, in order to retain as much of its
natural juices as possible.

Pork with Pickled Mustard Cabbage [SHUEN CHOY GEE YUK]

1 pound pickled cabbage
½ pound pork
1 wedge ginger size of quarter
1 teaspoon cornstarch with
    1 teaspoon water
½ teaspoon monosodium
    glutamate
Dash pepper
4 tablespoons vegetable oil
3 teaspoons sugar
½ teaspoon vinegar

½ teaspoon salt
¼ cup chicken stock or
    water

Marinade for pork:
1 teaspoon cornstarch
1 teaspoon light soy sauce
¼ teaspoon sugar
2 teaspoons sherry
¼ teaspoon vegetable oil

PREPARATION: Place pickled cabbage in brine for 20 minutes or so. Rinse thoroughly, squeeze dry, and slice into pieces ½ to ¾ inch wide. Using a medium flame, place cabbage in dry frying pan and stir for 4 minutes. This is to remove excess moisture. Set aside. Slice pork and add marinade. Smash ginger. Mix cornstarch solution, add monosodium and pepper. Set beside pan.

COOKING: Using a high flame, heat pan, add 3 tablespoons of oil and cabbage. Literally toast cabbage (this is to restore crunchy texture). At the same time sprinkle sugar and vinegar over cabbage. This will take about 2 minutes. Remove and set aside. Using a high flame, heat pan again and add 1 tablespoon of oil, ginger, salt, and pork. Stir pork until nearly done, about 3½ minutes, then add stock and cabbage. Thicken with cornstarch solution. *Serves 3.*

If you've never had this dish before, it is a must. It never fails to perk up my appetite. The trick to the success of this dish is restoring the texture of the pickled cabbage, which is, of course, soggy after all that soaking. Because of the difference in pickling from one batch to another, this recipe should only serve as a guide. The best way to do this dish is to taste the cabbage as you cook it. Sometimes you may not need as much sugar, other times you may want to omit the vinegar. The cabbage, upon cooking, should be crunchy in texture and taste sweet and sour. A delightful change from the usual dish.

Pork with Dried Oysters and Vegetables [HO SEE SOONG]

7 dried oysters
1 pound ground pork
8 Chinese mushrooms
8 water chestnuts
¼ cup bamboo shoots
2 stalks scallions
8 snow peas (optional)
¼ cup almonds
1 ounce ham
1 ounce Chinese parsley
2 cloves garlic
1 wedge ginger size of quarter
2 teaspoons cornstarch mixed
   with 2 teaspoons water
½ teaspoon sugar

½ teaspoon monosodium
   glutamate
1 tablespoon dark soy sauce
1 tablespoon oyster sauce
⅛ teaspoon pepper
2 tablespoons vegetable oil
½ teaspoon salt
¾ cup chicken stock or
   water

Marinade for pork:
1 teaspoon cornstarch
1 tablespoon sherry
2 teaspoons dark soy sauce
½ teaspoon sugar

PREPARATION: Soak oysters in water for 36 hours or until soft. Cut in half and wash thoroughly to remove all sand. Remove muscle and edge. Mince. Have pork ground or chop it, and add marinade. Soak mushrooms in cold water until soft, 15 or more minutes. Dice mushrooms, water chestnuts, and bamboo shoots. Mince scallions. String snow peas and cut diagonally into strips about an inch long. Chop almonds and shred ham. Wash parsley and pick off leaves or cut off stems. Mince garlic and ginger. Mix cornstarch solution and add sugar, monosodium, dark soy, oyster sauce, and pepper. Set beside pan.

COOKING: Using a high flame, heat pan and add 1 tablespoon of oil, salt, and ginger. Add oysters and stir for 1½ minutes, add ½ cup of stock and simmer until tender (approximately 20 minutes depending on oysters). Remove and set aside. Reheat pan and add 1 tablespoon of oil, garlic, and pork and stir for 1 minute. Add mushrooms, water chestnuts, bamboo shoots, oysters, and remainder of stock. Cover for 2½ minutes. Add scallions, snow peas, and cornstarch solution, and cook until cornstarch coats dish. Mix in almonds. Garnish with ham and parsley. *Serves 4.*

If you dislike seafood, exclude the oysters. This dish is usually served with freshly washed whole lettuce leaves. The diner spoons about 2 tablespoons of the dish, or enough to fill the center of the lettuce, and smears hoisin sauce over this. The edges of the leaf are folded over to cover the filling and eaten. This is called *sang choy bau,* or lettuce bun. I have never had this in a restaurant; this particular recipe happens to be one of my mother-in-law's specialties.

Sweet-and-Sour Pork Cubes [NIW GOO YUK]

½ pound pork tenderloin
1 large green pepper
¼ cup sliced carrots
2 rings pineapple
1 or 2 cloves garlic
1 tablespoon cornstarch mixed
   with 1 tablespoon water
¼ cup vinegar
½ cup water
Dash pepper
1½ teaspoons dark soy sauce

5 tablespoons sugar
½ teaspoon monosodium
   glutamate
3 tablespoons cornstarch or
   enough to dredge pork
1 tablespoon sherry
½ teaspoon salt
½ teaspoon Chinese bead
   molasses
3 cups oil

PREPARATION: Cut pork into ¾-inch squares. Wash and seed pepper and cut into 1-inch squares. Slice carrots diagonally. Parboil peppers (and carrots if you desire) for 1 minute. Slice pineapple into 1-inch pieces. Mince garlic very fine. Mix cornstarch solution and set beside pan. Mix vinegar, water, pepper, soy, sugar, monosodium, and minced garlic to make sweet-and-sour solution.

COOKING:

Step I: Roll pork cubes in cornstarch until dredged thoroughly. Add sherry slowly (about ½ teaspoon at a time), mixing the cubes evenly until each one is coated with a thick heavy paste. Heat deep-fat fryer or enough oil (3 cups) to 375 degrees. Drop in cubes. They will float when done. Leave in a few minutes longer until golden brown. Remove and drain on paper towel.

Step II: Using a high flame, heat pan and add salt and sweet-and-sour mixture. When it begins to boil, add cornstarch solution and stir until gravy thickens. Next add vegetables and pineapple and stir. Add pork and Chinese bead molasses and stir quickly but thoroughly until gravy coats all ingredients. *Serves 2 or 3.*

This dish when done right is heavenly. The pork should really be rolled into balls. The perfect dish is one in which the pork is completely coated with the sauce but is still crisp. The cornstarch makes a lighter, crisper coating than flour. Too often in inferior restaurants the pork has become soggy. One may add tomato wedges and onions as is done in some restaurants. I frankly think they add nothing to the dish. However, for added zest, slices of preserved ginger will do the trick. If you have tasted this dish, I need say no more. If you have not, you have not lived.

Deep-Fried Bean Curd with Pork and Vegetables
[DOW FU POK GEE YUK]

½ pound pork
4 deep-fried bean curd
½ cup bamboo shoots
½ cup celery
¼ cup Virginia ham
  (cooked)
10 medium-size Chinese
  mushrooms
1 clove garlic
2 teaspoons cornstarch mixed
  with 2 teaspoons water
½ teaspoon monosodium
  glutamate
Pinch sugar

1 tablespoon oyster sauce
Dash pepper
2 tablespoons vegetable oil
½ teaspoon salt
¾ cup chicken stock or
  water

Marinade for pork:
1 teaspoon cornstarch
1 teaspoon light soy sauce
2 teaspoons sherry
¼ teaspoon sugar
¼ teaspoon vegetable oil

PREPARATION: Shred pork and add marinade. Shred deep-fried bean curd, bamboo shoots, celery, and Virginia ham. Soak mushrooms in cold water for 15 minutes, or until soft, and shred. Mince garlic. Mix cornstarch solution and add monosodium, sugar, oyster sauce, and pepper. Set beside pan.

COOKING: Using a high flame, heat pan and add oil, salt and garlic. Next add pork and stir for 2 minutes. Next add bamboo shoots, mushrooms, and celery. Stir. Add stock and cover for 2 minutes. Add cornstarch solution and stir until it thickens, then add bean curd. Garnish with Virginia ham. *Serves 4.*

Deep-fried bean curd may be purchased in Chinese stores as *dow fu pok* or in Japanese stores as *aburage.* You may also deep fry it yourself. Just take one bean curd and slice into 4 squares. Heat oil for deep frying at 375 degrees. Fry bean curd until golden brown. If you deep fry your own, use 3 bean cakes and do not shred first.

Pressed Bean Curd with Pork and Vegetables [SHIANG GUR NYUK TZU]

½ pound pork
12 Chinese mushrooms
2 cups bamboo shoots
3 pressed bean cakes
4–6 small red peppers
2 cups green peppers
1 clove garlic
2 tablespoons vegetable oil
½ teaspoon salt
½ cup chicken stock or
  water

¼ teaspoon sugar
½ teaspoon monosodium
  glutamate

Marinade for pork:
1 teaspoon light soy sauce
1 teaspoon cornstarch
2 teaspoons sherry
¼ teaspoon sugar
¼ teaspoon vegetable oil

PREPARATION: Shred pork and add marinade. Soak mushrooms for 15 minutes in cold water or until soft. Shred mushrooms, bamboo shoots, and bean cakes. Wash and seed both red and green peppers. Shred both. (With red peppers, because of size, shred diagonally.) Mince garlic.

COOKING: Using a high flame, heat pan and add oil, salt, and garlic. Next add pork and stir for 1 minute. Next add all vegetables and stir. Add chicken stock and cover for 2½ minutes. Stir for another minute. Next add sugar, monosodium, and stir in bean cakes. *Serves 4.*

Pressed bean curd is called *dow fu kon*. It is preferred by some people because it is firmer and therefore texturally is easier to work with. If you cannot purchase it, make it in the following way: place bean cakes wrapped in cheesecloth or wax paper between two cutting boards. Weight top board with books, etc. Let stand for 5 hours or until bean curd becomes solid.

Twice-Cooked Pork [WEI GOON NYUK]

1 large pepper
1 leek (or 2 stalks scallions)
1 wedge ginger size of quarter
3 cloves garlic
1 tablespoon brown bean
   sauce
½ teaspoon monosodium
   glutamate
1 tablespoon water

1 teaspoon hoisin sauce
1 12-ounce strip of belly pork
   (fresh-cut pork that bacon
   or salt pork is made from)
2 tablespoons vegetable oil
½ teaspoon salt
2 teaspoons sherry
1 teaspoon Szechuan hot oil
½ teaspoon sugar

PREPARATION: Wash, seed, and cut pepper into 1-inch squares. Parboil for 1 minute. Cut top and bottom off leek, cut bottom in half lengthwise and wash thoroughly. Cut into 1-inch lengths. Mince ginger and garlic. Crush the beans in the brown sauce. Mix monosodium with water, hoisin sauce, and set beside pan.

COOKING:

Step I: Bring enough water to a boil to cover strip of pork. Place pork in pot and simmer or poach for 1 hour. Remove and cool. Cut against grain into slices 1/16 inch thick.

Step II: Using a high flame, heat pan and add oil, salt, garlic, ginger, and brown bean sauce. Next add leek and stir for 30 seconds. Add pork, sherry, sugar, and green pepper and stir for 1 minute. Add hoisin solution. Stir for 30 seconds or until whole dish is completely coated with it. Place on serving dish and sprinkle Szechuan oil on top. *Serves 2.*

If you like spicy food, you will love this dish. For an interesting variation try 2 tablespoons of subgum jheung (spicy *hoisin* sauce) instead of brown bean sauce.

Chicken with Pineapple [BOR LOR GAI PEEN]

½ pound boned chicken breast
¾ cup Chinese cabbage
¼ cup bamboo shoots
5 water chestnuts
6 Chinese mushrooms
4 slices pineapple
1 wedge ginger size of quarter
2 teaspoons cornstarch mixed with 2 teaspoons water

½ teaspoon monosodium glutamate
½ teaspoon light soy sauce
½ teaspoon sugar
2 tablespoons vegetable oil
1 teaspoon salt
¼ cup chicken stock or water
1 tablespoon sherry

PREPARATION: Bone breast of chicken and divide into thin uniform slices. Slice Chinese cabbage, bamboo shoots, and water chestnuts. Soak mushrooms in cold water for 15 minutes, or until soft, and slice into strips. Cut pineapple into 1-inch squares. Smash ginger. Mix cornstarch solution and add monosodium, soy, and sugar. Set beside pan.

COOKING: Using a high flame, heat pan and add 1 tablespoon of oil, ½ teaspoon of salt, and ginger. Add Chinese cabbage, mushrooms, bamboo shoots, and water chestnuts. Stir for 30 seconds. Next add stock and cover for 2 minutes. Remove and set aside. Reheat pan and add remaining oil and ½ teaspoon of salt. Next add chicken and flatten against sides of pan. Add sherry and cook for 1 minute or until color changes from pink to white. Turn over and cook other side to nearly done, then add vegetables and pineapple. When stock boils, add cornstarch solution and stir until thick. *Serves 2.*

The chicken in this recipe may be leftover roast chicken or chicken breasts that have been poached for 20 minutes. In that case the chicken would be thrown in at the end with the pineapple. I personally think it is much tastier if you do it the way the recipe indicates. Chicken should never be overcooked to the point where the meat is dry and stringy and worse yet until it crumbles in your mouth. Rather it should be cooked just done, where the meat is tender, juicy, and velvety.

Chicken with Mushrooms [MOU GOO GAI PEEN]

½ pound boned chicken
breast
¾ cup Chinese cabbage
¼ cup bamboo shoots
5 water chestnuts
½ cup canned or fresh
mushrooms
12 snow peas
1 wedge ginger size of quarter
2 teaspoons cornstarch mixed
with 2 teaspoons water

Dash pepper
½ teaspoon monosodium
glutamate
¼ teaspoon sugar
2 tablespoons vegetable oil
1 teaspoon salt
¼ cup chicken stock or
water
1 tablespoon sherry

PREPARATION: Bone breast and divide into thin uniform slices. Slice Chinese cabbage, bamboo shoots, water chestnuts, and mushrooms if fresh ones are used. String snow peas and if very large cut in half, using a diagonal cut. Smash ginger. Mix cornstarch solution and add pepper, monosodium, and sugar. Set beside pan.

COOKING: Using a high flame, heat pan and add 1 tablespoon of oil, ½ teaspoon of salt, and ginger. Add Chinese cabbage, mushrooms, bamboo shoots, and water chestnuts. Stir for 30 seconds. Next add stock and cover for 2 minutes. Remove and set aside. Reheat pan and add remainder of oil and salt. Add chicken and flatten against sides of pan. Add sherry and cook for 1 minute or until color changes from pink to white. Turn over and cook other side until nearly done, then add vegetables and snow peas. When stock reaches boil, add cornstarch solution and stir until thick. *Serves 2.*

This is a delicate, subtle dish. The sauce is a white sauce, so no soy is used. You will notice that the method of cooking is identical with the preceding recipe.

Chicken with Asparagus [LO SHON CHOW GAI]

½ boned spring chicken
1 pound asparagus
2 tablespoons black beans
2 cloves garlic
2 teaspoons cornstarch mixed
    with 2 teaspoons water
¼ teaspoon sugar

½ teaspoon monosodium
    glutamate
Dash pepper
2 tablespoons vegetable oil
1 teaspoon salt
½ cup chicken stock
1 tablespoon sherry

PREPARATION: Cut chicken into uniform thin slices. Slice stems of asparagus diagonally into paper-thin slices. Leave tips whole if very young, or cut in half if older. Rinse black beans and mince. Mince garlic. Mix cornstarch and add sugar, monosodium, and pepper. Set beside pan.

COOKING: Using a high flame, heat pan and add 1 tablespoon of oil, ½ teaspoon of salt, ½ of the black beans, and garlic. When odor of beans becomes pungent (about 30 seconds), add asparagus. Stir for 30 seconds and add stock. Cover for 2 minutes or until asparagus is half cooked. Remove and set aside. Next reheat pan and add remaining oil. Add chicken and stir for 30 seconds. Flatten against pan and add sherry. When chicken is done color will change (about 2 or 3 minutes depending on amount of chicken). Turn over and cook other side and add asparagus. Stir for another minute. Add cornstarch solution and stir until gravy thickens. *Serves 4.*

This is a delicious way to serve both chicken and asparagus. The two seem to go together so well. Leaving out the black beans, this is a basic recipe for chicken with one vegetable. The chicken may also be cut into chunks: in that case it would be a *kow* dish (meaning chunk) rather than a *peen* dish (meaning slice).

Curried Chicken [GAR LAY GAI]

½ boned spring chicken
1 onion
1 teaspoon cornstarch mixed
  with 1 teaspoon water
½ teaspoon sugar
½ teaspoon monosodium
  glutamate

Dash pepper
5 tablespoons curry powder
½ cup chicken stock or
  water
½ teaspoon salt

PREPARATION: Slice chicken into uniform 1-inch pieces. Cut onion into half rings. Mix cornstarch solution and add sugar, monosodium, and pepper. Set beside pan.

COOKING: Using a low flame, stir fry or brown curry powder and onion until odor of curry is pungent. Add chicken and stir, next add stock and salt and bring flame up to high. Cover. Cook until chicken is done, about 6 minutes, stirring occasionally. Stir in cornstarch solution and mix until gravy thickens. Serves 2.

Diced Chicken with Vegetables [GAI DING]

½ boned spring chicken
1 wedge ginger size of quarter
2 teaspoons cornstarch mixed
  with 2 teaspoons water
¼ teaspoon sugar
½ teaspoon monosodium
  glutamate
Dash pepper
¼ cup almonds
5 tablespoons salt
2 tablespoons vegetable oil

1½ teaspoons salt
1 cup Chinese cabbage
½ cup canned mushrooms
4 water chestnuts
¼ cup celery
½ cup bamboo shoots
¼ cup chicken stock or
  water
2 teaspoons sherry
12 snow peas

PREPARATION: Dice chicken into pieces approximately ½ inch square. Dice all vegetables. Smash wedge of ginger. Mix cornstarch solution and add sugar, monosodium, and pepper. Set beside pan.

COOKING: Using a high flame and a dry frying pan, toast almonds in 5 tablespoons of salt. Remove and set aside. Reheat pan and add 1 tablespoon of oil, 1 teaspoon of salt, and ginger. Next add Chinese cabbage, mushrooms, water chestnuts, celery, and bamboo shoots. Stir for 30 seconds. Add stock and cover for 2 minutes. Remove and set aside. Heat pan and add remainder of oil and ½ teaspoon of salt. Add chicken and sherry. Stir for 2 minutes. Add vegetables and snow peas. Stir for 30 seconds and bring stock to a boil. Add cornstarch solution and stir until thick. Garnish with almonds. *Serves 2 or 3.*

This is a basic recipe for diced chicken with mixed vegetables. Almonds may be deep fried instead of toasted. For chicken with walnuts, substitute walnuts for almonds. The next recipe is basically the same but spicier because of added spices and sauces.

Chicken with Peanuts [KUNG PO GAI]

½ spring chicken
5 Chinese mushrooms
2 stalks scallions
1 clove garlic
1 tablespoon brown bean sauce
2 tablespoons water
1 wedge ginger size of acorn
1 teaspoon cornstarch mixed with 1 teaspoon water

½ teaspoon Chinese bead molasses
¼ teaspoon cayenne pepper or to taste ·
2 tablespoons vegetable oil
1 tablespoon sherry
⅓ cup roasted peanuts

PREPARATION: Bone chicken and dice into pieces ⅜ inch square. Soak Chinese mushrooms for approximately 15 minutes in cold water, or until soft. Dice mushrooms. Mince scallions. Mince garlic. Mash brown beans with handle of choy doh and add water. Smash wedge of ginger. Mix corn-starch solution and add bead molasses and cayenne pepper. Set beside pan.

COOKING: Using a high flame, heat pan and add oil, ginger, and garlic. Add chicken and sherry. Stir for 1 minute and add mushrooms. After ½ minute add brown bean sauce solution, scallions, and peanuts. Stir and add cornstarch solution. Dish is done when cornstarch thickens and coats ingredients. Also, all ingredients should be coated evenly with brown bean sauce and molasses. *Serves 2 or 3.*

This is a spicy dish that is a rich dark brown in color. Actually, I have cut down the amount of cayenne pepper that really goes into the dish, but if you like spicy food by all means add more.

Chicken with Oyster Sauce [HO YAU GAI]

½ spring chicken
2 stalks scallions
2 cloves garlic
1 wedge ginger size of acorn
4 tablespoons oyster sauce
1 teaspoon light soy sauce
1 tablespoon sherry
2 teaspoons cornstarch mixed with 2 teaspoons water

1 teaspoon sugar
½ teaspoon monosodium glutamate
Dash pepper
2 tablespoons vegetable oil
½ cup chicken stock or water

PREPARATION: Chop spring chicken with bones into pieces 1 inch by 1½ inches. Cut tops of scallions into pieces 1 inch long and shred bottoms into inch-long shreds. Mince garlic. Smash ginger. Mix oyster sauce, soy, and sherry. Mix corn-starch solution and add sugar, monosodium, and pepper. Set beside pan.

COOKING: Using a high flame, add oil, garlic, and ginger. Add chicken and stir for 4 minutes or until brown. Next add oyster sauce mixture and stir until chicken is completely coated. Add stock, cover, and turn flame to simmer. Simmer for 4 minutes or until tender, adding more stock if necessary. Uncover, turn flame to high, and add cornstarch solution and scallions. Stir until thick. *Serves 2 or 3.*

Chicken with Brown Bean Sauce [GUNG BAU GEE DING]

½ boned spring chicken
1 tablespoon cornstarch
1 tablespoon sherry
1 teaspoon salt
2 tablespoons vegetable oil
7 Chinese mushrooms
⅓ cup bamboo shoots
1 green pepper
1 clove garlic
2 tablespoons brown bean sauce

1 wedge ginger size of quarter
1 teaspoon cornstarch mixed with 1 teaspoon water
½ teaspoon sugar
½ teaspoon monosodium glutamate
½ cup chicken stock or water
1 tablespoon Szechuan hot oil

PREPARATION: Dice chicken. Coat with 1 tablespoon cornstarch, sherry, and ½ teaspoon salt. Deep fry in oil at 375 degrees until brown. Drain and set aside. Meanwhile soak mushrooms in cold water for 15 minutes, or until soft. Dice mushrooms, bamboo shoots, and green pepper. Mince garlic and mash brown bean sauce with handle of choy doh. Smash wedge of ginger. Mix cornstarch solution and add sugar and monosodium. Set beside pan.

COOKING: Using a high flame, add oil, ½ teaspoon of salt, ginger, and garlic. Next add all vegetables and stir for 30 seconds. Add stock and cover for 1 minute. Next stir in chicken and brown bean sauce. When dish is thoroughly coated, add cornstarch solution and stir until thick. Sprinkle Szechuan hot oil over top. *Serves 2 or 3.*

Sometimes the Chinese deep fry their chicken before stir frying it because they feel it gives the dish one more dimension of taste and texture. Coating the chicken is the secret, and occasionally egg white is also used. This gives the chicken a smoother texture.

Sweet-and-Sour Chicken Bones [TIEM SHUEN GAI GWOT]

Whole carcass of boned chicken or ½ chicken
1 large green pepper
¼ cup sliced carrots
2 rings pineapple
1–2 cloves garlic
1 tablespoon cornstarch mixed with 1 tablespoon water
¼ cup vinegar
½ cup water
Dash pepper

1½ teaspoons dark soy sauce
5 tablespoons sugar
½ teaspoon monosodium glutamate
4 tablespoons cornstarch or enough to dredge chicken
1–2 tablespoons sherry
1 teaspoon salt
3 cups vegetable oil
½ teaspoon Chinese bead molasses

PREPARATIONS: Chop carcass or chicken with bones into 1-inch pieces. Wash and seed pepper and cut into 1-inch squares. Slice carrots diagonally. Parboil pepper (and carrots if you desire) for 1 minute. Slice pineapple into 1-inch pieces. Mince garlic very fine. Mix cornstarch solution and set beside pan. Mix sweet-and-sour solution: vinegar, water, ½ teaspoon salt, pepper, soy, sugar, monosodium, and minced garlic.

COOKING:

Step I: Add 4 tablespoons of cornstarch, sherry, and ½ teaspoon of salt to chicken bones or chicken. All pieces should be evenly coated with thick damp paste. Heat deep fat fryer or enough oil (3 cups) to 375 degrees. Drop in chicken.

Pieces will float when done. Leave in a few minutes longer until golden brown. Remove and drain on paper towel.

Step II: Using a high flame, heat pan and add sweet-and-sour mixture. When it reaches a boil, add cornstarch solution and stir until gravy thickens. Next add vegetables and pineapple and stir. Add chicken and Chinese bead molasses and stir quickly but thoroughly until gravy coats all ingredients. *Serves 2 or 3.*

The Chinese bead molasses is added to make the sauce richer brown in color.

One Chicken Three Flavors [YAT GAI SAM MEI]

Using one chicken one can make 3 separate dishes for a complete meal.

1. Use the chicken liver, gizzard, and neck to make soup.
2. Use breast and other pieces of boned meat to make Chicken with Pineapple (p. 83), or Chicken with Mushrooms (p. 84), or Chicken with Asparagus (p. 85).
3. Use the bones and tips of wings to make Sweet-and-Sour Chicken Bones (p. 90).

Lobster Cantonese [CHOW LUNG HAR]

1½–2 *pounds lobster*
2 *tablespoons black beans*
1–2 *cloves garlic*
1 *stalk scallion*
1 *egg*
1 *tablespoon cornstarch mixed with 1 tablespoon water*
¼ *teaspoon sugar*

¼ *teaspoon monosodium glutamate*
Dash pepper
2 *tablespoons vegetable oil*
½ *teaspoon salt*
1 *paper-thin slice ginger*
1½ *cups chicken stock or water*
½ *pound ground pork*

PREPARATION: Clean and chop lobster into 8 pieces. (Have butcher do it but be sure lobster is alive when he does it.) Rinse black beans and mince. Mince garlic and scallion. Slightly beat egg. Mix cornstarch solution and add sugar, monosodium, and pepper. Set beside pan.

COOKING: Using a high flame, heat pan and add oil, salt, black beans, garlic, and ginger. After 30 seconds or when pungent smell of beans becomes evident, add pork and stir for 45 seconds. Next add lobster and stock. Stir and cover for 5 minutes or until lobster is done. You will know this because the shell will turn fiery red and the meat will turn from a translucent white to a chalk white. The pork should be done by this time also. Thicken gravy with cornstarch solution and stir in scallion. Just as you turn flame off stir in beaten egg. *Serves 3.*

This is a marvelous way to do lobster. The egg is stirred in at the end really to give the whole dish color. It should give the gravy a yellowish appearance, a contrast to the black beans, red lobster, and green scallion. Therefore, be certain that the egg does not really cook, because it will then turn white. The lobster should also not be overcooked as it will become tough and stringy. For a variation substitute shrimp for lobster in the recipe.

Butterfly Shrimp [WOR TEAP HAR]

12 *large shrimp*
12 *thin slices Smithfield ham*
3 *slices lean bacon*
2 *eggs*
3 *tablespoons flour*
1 *large onion*
¼ *cup catsup*
3 *tablespoons Worcestershire sauce*
2 *teaspoons sugar*

⅓ *cup water*
1 *teaspoon monosodium glutamate*
2 *teaspoons cornstarch mixed with 2 teaspoons water*
½ *teaspoon dark soy sauce*
Dash pepper
1 *clove garlic*
3 *tablespoons vegetable oil*
½ *teaspoon salt*

PREPARATION: Remove shell of shrimp with exception of the tail. Clean and remove vein. Cut halfway to three-quarters through back and flatten with light tap of flat surface of knife. Cut ham and bacon into 12 pieces 1 inch by 2 inches or to fit flattened surface of shrimp. Using a wire whisk, mix batter of flour and eggs until the consistency is like thick molasses or heavy glue. The batter will form balls or drops at this stage when you test it with a fork. (You may need more flour or less egg.) Dip one side of ham into batter and apply on shrimp. Do the same with the bacon, so that each shrimp will have a piece of ham dipped in batter and a piece of bacon dipped in batter placed over the ham. Cut onion into half rings. Mix catsup, Worcestershire, sugar, water, and monosodium. Mix cornstarch solution and add soy and pepper. Set beside pan. Mince garlic.

COOKING: Using a high flame, add 2 tablespoons of vegetable oil and place shrimp bacon side down in pan. Fry for 2 minutes. Cover for 30 seconds. Next reduce flame slightly and turn shrimp over. Fry for 2 minutes or until done. Remove and set aside on paper towel. Next reheat pan and stir fry onion for 2 minutes. Line bottom of serving dish with onion. Reheat pan adding remaining oil, salt, and garlic. Add catsup mixture and bring to boil. Thicken with cornstarch solution. Arrange shrimp over onions and pour sauce over shrimp. *Serves 2 or 3.*

You may use thin slices of boiled ham instead of Smithfield ham.

Shrimp with Tomato Sauce [CARE JUP HAR]

1 pound shrimp
1 clove garlic
1 teaspoon cornstarch mixed
  with 1 teaspoon water
Dash pepper
½ teaspoon monosodium
  glutamate
1 teaspoon light soy sauce

1 teaspoon sugar
2 tablespoons vegetable oil
½ teaspoon salt
1 thin slice ginger
2 teaspoons sherry
¼ cup chicken stock or
  water
½ cup catsup

PREPARATION: Wash and clean shrimp, removing vein. Mince garlic. Mix cornstarch solution and add pepper, monosodium, soy, and sugar. Set beside pan.

COOKING: Using a high flame, heat pan and add oil, salt, ginger, and garlic. Next add shrimp and stir for 30 seconds. Add sherry and stock. Cook for 2 minutes or until shrimp change color. Add catsup and stir until entire dish is coated evenly. Next thicken gravy with cornstarch solution. *Serves 2 or 3.*

Shrimp with Bean Sprouts [ARE CHOY HAR]

½ pound shrimp
½ pound bean sprouts
1 clove garlic
1 teaspoon cornstarch mixed
  with 1 teaspoon water
¼ teaspoon sugar
½ teaspoon monosodium
  glutamate

Dash pepper
2 tablespoons vegetable oil
1 teaspoon salt
1 thin slice ginger
2 teaspoons sherry
¼ cup chicken stock or
  water

PREPARATION: Wash and clean shrimp, removing vein. Wash bean sprouts and if you have the patience remove tails. Mince garlic. Mix cornstarch solution and add sugar, monosodium, and pepper. Set beside pan.

COOKING: Using a high flame, heat pan and add 1 tablespoon of oil, ½ teaspoon of salt, and ginger. Add shrimp and stir for 30 seconds. Next add sherry and stir for 1½ minutes. Remove and set aside. Reheat pan and add remainder of salt, oil, and garlic. Add bean sprouts and stir. Next add chicken stock and cover for 2 minutes. Add shrimp, and when stock reaches boiling point add cornstarch solution. Stir until thick. *Serves 2.*

This is a basic shrimp-with-one-vegetable dish. You may use green peppers, peas, onions, or many other vegetables. Remember that cooking times will vary, and just use color as your main guide.

Curried Shrimp [GAR LAY HAR]

½ pound shrimp	Dash pepper
1 onion	1 tablespoon vegetable oil
2 teaspoons cornstarch mixed with 2 teaspoons water	¾ teaspoon salt
½ teaspoon sugar	2 teaspoons sherry
1 teaspoon monosodium glutamate	3 tablespoons curry
	½ cup chicken stock or water

PREPARATION: Wash and clean shrimp, removing vein. Slice onion into half rings. Mix cornstarch solution and add sugar, monosodium, and pepper. Set beside pan.

COOKING: Using a high flame, add oil, salt, and shrimp. Stir for 30 seconds. Add sherry and stir for 1½ minutes or until shrimp changes color. Remove and set aside. Clean pan. Using a low flame, add curry powder to dry pan and stir for ½ minute. Next add onions and continue stirring until odor of curry fills kitchen. Do this for at least a minute. Next add shrimp and stock, and turn flame to high. Bring mixture to a boil, and if onion is not done enough to your taste cook a little longer. Add cornstarch solution and thicken gravy. *Serves 2.*

The amount of curry powder indicated in the recipe is relative. If you like your curry dishes really hot, increase the amount.

Diced Shrimp with Vegetables [CHOW HAR DING]

½ *pound shrimp*
5 *Chinese mushrooms*
1 *cup diced Chinese cabbage*
10 *water chestnuts*
¼ *cup bamboo shoots*
12 *snow peas*
1 *clove garlic*
2 *teaspoons cornstarch mixed with 2 teaspoons water*
¼ *teaspoon sugar*

½ *teaspoon monosodium glutamate*
Dash pepper
2 *tablespoons vegetable oil*
1 *teaspoon salt*
¼ *cup button mushrooms*
¼ *cup frozen peas*
¼ *cup chicken stock or water*

PREPARATION: Wash and clean shrimp, removing vein. Boil for 1½ minutes. Rinse in cold water and dice. Soak Chinese mushrooms in cold water for 15 minutes or until soft. Dice all mushrooms, cabbage, water chestnuts, bamboo shoots, and snow peas. Mince garlic. Mix cornstarch solution and add sugar, monosodium, and pepper. Set beside pan.

COOKING: Using a high flame, heat pan and add oil, salt, and garlic. Add Chinese cabbage, water chestnuts, bamboo shoots, two kinds of mushrooms, and frozen peas. Stir for 30 seconds. Next add stock and cover for 1½ minutes. Next add snow peas and shrimp. Stir in cornstarch solution and turn flame off when gravy thickens. *Serves 2 or 3.*

This dish is really delicious if the tiny baby shrimp are used. These are sweet and juicy but are available only in specialty shops frozen. In this case it would not be necessary to dice them. Shrimp with walnuts is a variation of this dish. Just add walnuts as the flame is being turned off.

Sliced Fish with Chinese Vegetables [YU PEEN]

2 pounds pike or sea bass
1 teaspoon cornstarch
½ teaspoon light soy sauce
½ teaspoon sherry
8 cloud's ears (¼ cup)
4 paper-thin slices ginger
¼ pound Chinese cabbage
3 water chestnuts
12 snow peas
1 teaspoon cornstarch mixed
   with 1 teaspoon water

¼ teaspoon sugar
Dash pepper
½ teaspoon monosodium
   glutamate
2 tablespoons vegetable oil
¾ teaspoon salt
½ cup chicken stock or
   water

PREPARATION: Have butcher fillet fish for you. You will probably end up with actually ¾ pounds of fish fillet. Prepare fillet in slices ¼ inch thin or more. Slice across grain into slices approximately 2 inches long, leaving original width. Coat slices with 1 teaspoon of cornstarch, soy, and sherry. Soak cloud's ears for 15 minutes in water or until soft. Wash and slice ginger as thin as possible. Wash and slice Chinese cabbage diagonally. Slice water chestnuts thin. String snow peas and cut in halves. Mix cornstarch solution and add sugar, pepper, and monosodium. Set beside pan.

COOKING: Using a high flame, add 1 tablespoon of oil and ½ teaspoon of salt. Add Chinese cabbage and water chestnuts. Next add stock and cover for 2 minutes. Remove and set aside. Reheat pan, add 1 tablespoon of oil, the ginger, and ¼ teaspoon of salt. When pan is red hot, add fish and stir for 45 seconds. Next add Chinese cabbage, water chestnuts, cloud's ears, and snow peas, and stir. When stock reaches boil, thicken with cornstarch solution. Serves 3 or 4.

You may substitute broccoli for Chinese cabbage and leave

out all the other vegetables. Cooking time will be longer.
Fillet of lemon sole can be used but it will have a tendency
to crumble and break with stir frying. You may also cut the
fish into chunks. The dish would then be called *Chow Yu
Kow*. *Kow* indicates the fish is cut into chunks.

Sweet-and-Sour Fish [TIEM SHUEN YU]

1 *egg*
5 *tablespoons flour*
1 *pound sea bass*
1 *small green pepper*
1 *small carrot*
2 *rings pineapple*
5 *slices ginger*
1½ *cups water*
¼ *cup vinegar*
5 *tablespoons sugar*
1 *teaspoon dark soy sauce*

Dash pepper
1 *tablespoon sherry*
½ *teaspoon Chinese bead
   molasses*
2 *tablespoons cornstarch
   mixed with 2 tablespoons
   water*
½ *teaspoon monosodium
   glutamate*
1 *tablespoon vegetable oil*
¾ *teaspoon salt*

PREPARATION: Mix egg and flour to make smooth batter. Coat
fish thoroughly with batter. Deep fry in boiling oil 4 minutes
on each side. Meanwhile shred green pepper, carrot, and pineapple. Wash ginger and slice thinly. Fish should be done at
this point. Remove to warm serving platter. Mix sweet-and-
sour solution: water, vinegar, sugar, soy, pepper, sherry, and
bead molasses. Mix cornstarch solution and monosodium.
Set beside pan.

COOKING: Using a high flame, heat pan and add oil, salt and
ginger. Next add carrot, green pepper, and pineapple and stir.
When vegetables are half done (30 seconds) add sweet-and-
sour solution and bring to boil. Thicken with cornstarch solution. Pour this over fish and serve. *Serves 2*.

The reader has probably noticed that all the sweet-and-sour
dishes are not pure chow recipes but combine deep frying
with stir frying.

MASTERING THE METHOD
OF *JING*

Wet steaming is probably the Chinese housewife's favorite method of cooking because it is simple and doesn't require constant attention. The original Chinese steamer is called a *jing loong* and is made of bamboo. These steamers were made to be stacked on a wok. However, jing loongs are not only very difficult to obtain in this country but also present a storage problem, as they are rather cumbersome and, having no handles, cannot be hung. Although they make an attractive conversation piece they are an impractical luxury in any kitchen, strictly from the point of view of storage and durability. The ones that are more commonly sold are made of aluminum and come in two parts. The lower part is a round

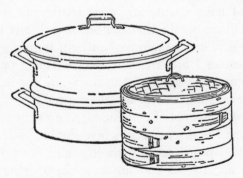

Jing loong—bamboo and aluminum

container for water, and the upper part resembles a perforated double boiler or flat colander. The actual steamers or perforated sections are made to stack one on top of the other so that several dishes can be steamed at the same time. However, one doesn't need to go through considerable expense to obtain all the equipment, for the clever housewife can improvise with what she has available. If one has a wok, a rack may be used with the deep cover of the wok. If a rack isn't avail-

Steaming, using a rack (Dotted line indicates water level)

able, wooden chopsticks or two identical pieces of wood can be wedged in to form a platform on which the dish can rest. If you don't have a wok, any deep frying pan with an adequate lid will do or, for that matter, so will any deep pot as long as the dish can be removed without burning yourself. In dire emergencies I find that my electric frying pan, which is quite deep, makes a wonderful steamer, and the beauty of this is that it leaves a burner free on your range.

The Western school of cooking often uses the term "steaming" to mean the dry method where double boilers are used, but the actual principle of steaming—and the principle used in Chinese cooking—is cooking in a chamber of live steam. This method saves time and labor and also preserves food nutriments and flavor. The food is cooked on the platter or dish it is going to be served in so at no time does it touch another container or utensil and, therefore, not a single drop of nutriment is lost.

These are the rules that govern this method of cooking:

1. It is important that the chamber or pot be filled with live steam, so one must be absolutely certain the water is boiling vigorously before he places the dish in to be steamed.
2. The water level in the pot should never be above the bottom of the dish. This is taken care of automatically if one has steamers.
3. The flame, which initially is on high to bring the water to the boiling point, should be turned to medium once the steaming process has been started. This insures against complete evaporation, a burned pot, and a ruined dish.
4. The meats cooked in this way should be of prime quality.
5. The food is cooked on the service plate so the dish goes from the steamer directly to the table.
6. It is important that the food that is steamed be just underdone because the plate remains hot for quite a few minutes after it is removed from the steamer, and the food continues to cook.
7. Food prepared in this way should be eaten promptly and not be kept waiting.

It has been my experience that this method of cooking is invaluable for people recovering from gastro-intestinal ailments and also for infants. It is easily digestible and rich in natural flavors.

Steamed Acorn Squash

> *Whole acorn squash (about 1 pound)*
> *2 pats butter*
> *Salt and pepper to taste*

PREPARATION: Wash acorn squash and cut into halves. Remove seeds.

COOKING: Place in steamer and steam until tender. Time depends on size of squash. A squash about 1 pound requires about 25 minutes of steaming. When done, serve immediately with pats of butter and add salt and pepper at table to taste. *Serves 2 to 3.*

This is strictly my invention, using the Chinese method of cooking, but is worth trying. Steaming prevents loss of juices and flavors and really makes this vegetable delicious this way.

Steamed Asparagus [JING LO SHUN]

1 *pound asparagus*
2 *wedges lemon*
Salt and pepper to taste

PREPARATION: Wash asparagus and cut off tough ends, about 2 inches. Place on dish (preferably an oval one, which is much more attractive).

COOKING: Steam about 5 minutes, until done. Asparagus turns a bright green. Remove before color starts to deteriorate and get darker. Serve immediately, garnished with wedges of lemon, and add salt and pepper to taste. *Serves 2 to 3.*

This again is strictly an American dish, using the Chinese method. With green vegetables, color should be the main guide. Try cooking corn this way.

Steamed Ground Beef [JING NGOW YUK]

1 *pound ground beef*
3 *scallions*
1 *egg*
2 *teaspoons cornstarch*
½ *teaspoon sesame seed oil*
   (*optional*)
1 *teaspoon sherry*
¾ *teaspoon salt*
2 *teaspoons dark soy sauce*
½ *teaspoon sugar*
¼ *teaspoon pepper*
1 *clove garlic*

PREPARATION: Mince scallions and chop garlic very fine. Mix all ingredients together.

COOKING: Place dish in steamer and steam for 12 minutes. Skim off excess fat and serve immediately. *Serves 3.*

This is strictly an invention of my own, cooked the Chinese way. For a variation add diced Chinese mushrooms.

Steamed Beef with Tea Melon [CHA QUAR JING NGOW YUK]

½ pound beef	Marinade for beef:
8 tea melons	*½ teaspoon cornstarch*
1 ball salted turnip	*½ teaspoon light soy sauce*
	1 teaspoon sherry
	¼ teaspoon sugar
	¼ teaspoon vegetable oil

PREPARATION: Slice beef. Slice tea melon; if mixed with ginger, slice pieces of preserved ginger also. Wash salted turnip and slice. Mix marinade into beef. Mix in tea melon and salted turnip.

COOKING: Place in steamer for 4 minutes or until meat is nearly done and serve immediately. Meat will continue cooking at table. *Serves 2.*

The meat in this dish should be on the rare side to insure tenderness.

Steamed Meat Patties [SHU MEI]

1 ounce Chinese mushrooms (about 5 small)
2 stalks scallions
6 water chestnuts
2 ounces roast pork (about 5 slices see page 155)
2 slices Virginia ham (boiled ham may be substituted)
¾ pound ground pork

3 tablespoons cornstarch
½ teaspoon sesame oil
½ teaspoon salt
½ teaspoon sugar
Dash pepper
1 teaspoon monosodium glutamate
1 tablespoon sherry

Wrapping:
12 wonton skins

PREPARATION: Soak mushrooms in cold water until soft (about 15 minutes). Mince very finely mushrooms, scallions, water chestnuts, roast pork, and ham. Mix all ingredients with pork.

WRAPPING: Use a small butter knife and spread mixture thinly and evenly over entire wonton skin. Holding the skin in the palm of the left hand, use the butter knife as a guide and place it directly in center of the skin. Then bring skin together around the knife. Using the thumb and index finger of the left hand, press lightly about ½ inch from loose ends of wonton skin. This motion is aided by turning the knife which is still inserted. This forms a round pouch on the closed end of the patties followed by a neck and the open loose ends, much like a flower or an incomplete figure 8. The patties are then placed on a dish which has been lightly greased with vegetable oil.

COOKING: Steam for 25 minutes. Serve immediately. Good if dipped in hoisin sauce or mustard and soy sauce. Serves 4.

For a more elegant variation, the filling can be used to stuff large Chinese mushrooms. The filling may also be varied by using shrimp combined with pork.

Pearl Balls [LOR MEI JING NGOW YUK]

1 cup glutinous rice
2 thin slices ginger
¼ cup onion
1 pound ground beef
1 tablespoon cornstarch
2 egg whites

½ teaspoon sugar
1 tablespoon dark soy sauce
½ teaspoon salt
1 teaspoon sherry
Dash pepper
1 tablespoon vegetable oil

PREPARATION: Soak glutinous rice at least 2 or 3 hours. Drain and set aside. Meanwhile mince ginger and onion very fine. Add all ingredients to ground beef, being careful not to handle beef too much as it loses its natural juices. Use a tablespoon and form into balls. Roll in glutinous rice.

COOKING: Place on flat plate lined with a damp napkin and steam for 20 minutes. Serve immediately. *Serves 3.*
This dish appeals not only to the taste but to the eye. It should be served with mustard and soy sauce.

Steamed Pork with Salted Turnip [CHUNG CHOY JING GEE YUK]

1 pound pork
4 balls salted turnip
1 teaspoon cornstarch
1 tablespoon sherry
½ teaspoon sugar

½ teaspoon light soy sauce
¼ teaspoon salt
1 tablespoon vegetable oil
Dash pepper

PREPARATION: Slice pork. Wash salted turnip and shred. Mix all ingredients into pork, then add salted turnip.

COOKING: Steam for 15 minutes. Pork is done when it changes color. Serve immediately. *Serves 3.*

Steamed Ground Pork with Salted Duck's Egg
[HAHM DUN JING GEE YUK]

6 water chestnuts	2 teaspoons sherry
1 salted duck's egg	½ teaspoon salt
1 egg	½ teaspoon sugar
1 pound ground pork	Dash pepper
1 teaspoon cornstarch	½ teaspoon light soy sauce
½ teaspoon monosodium glutamate	2 teaspoons vegetable oil

PREPARATION: Mince water chestnuts very fine. Break duck's egg in separate dish. Add white of duck's egg, whole egg beaten, and all other ingredients with pork. Break duck's egg yolk with fork and spread over top of dish.

COOKING: Steam for 20 minutes. Serve immediately. Dish is especially good if served with mustard and soy sauce. *Serves 3.*

For a variation of this dish, try substituting ¼ cup minced Smithfield ham for the salted duck's egg. Mix ham with pork and steam. Another variation is Chinese pork sausage (*lop chong*), substituting 2 pork sausages for salted duck's egg. Mince pork sausage and mix with pork.

Spare-ribs with Black Bean Sauce [DOW SEE PAI QUOT]

1 pound spare-ribs	1 tablespoon vegetable oil
3 tablespoons black beans	2 teaspoons sherry
4 or 5 cloves garlic (approximately 1 tablespoon)	3 tablespoons sugar
	½ teaspoon cornstarch
1 stalk scallion	2 tablespoons chicken stock or water
1 teaspoon salt	2 tablespoons vinegar

PREPARATION: Have butcher chop spare-ribs into inch-long pieces. Place ribs in boiling water for 4 minutes. Rinse with cold water and drain. This removes excess fat. Rinse black beans and mince. Mince garlic very fine. Cut scallion in ½-inch-long pieces. Mix all ingredients together and pour over ribs.

COOKING: Steam for 30 to 45 minutes or until tender. Serve immediately. *Serves 2 or 3.*
   Delicious!

Steamed Chicken I [JING GAI]

1 *pound spring chicken* (½ *a chicken*)	Marinade for chicken:
1 *ounce Chinese mushrooms* (*about 5*)	1½ *teaspoons vegetable oil*
¼ *cup bamboo shoots*	1 *teaspoon dark soy sauce*
4 *water chestnuts*	1 *teaspoon sherry*
	Dash of pepper
	½ *teaspoon sugar*
	½ *teaspoon cornstarch*

PREPARATION: Chop chicken into bite-size pieces. Mix in marinade. Soak mushrooms in cold water until soft (about 15 minutes). Rinse and shred. Slice bamboo shoots and water chestnuts. Mix into chicken.

COOKING: Steam for 7 minutes, stirring occasionally. Serve immediately. *Serves 2 or 3.*

Steamed Chicken II [JING GAI]

2 *pounds spring chicken*	Marinade for chicken:
4 *stalks scallions*	1 *tablespoon light soy sauce*
4 *thin slices ginger (about 2*	2 *teaspoons sherry*
teaspoons)	1 *teaspoon cornstarch*
1 *ball salted turnip*	2 *teaspoons vegetable oil*
2 *ounces Chinese mushrooms*	½ *teaspoon sugar*
(about 10)	Generous *dash pepper*

PREPARATION: Chop chicken into bite-size pieces. Mix in marinade. Mince scallions and shred ginger. Wash salted turnip and shred. Soak mushrooms in cold water until soft (about 15 minutes). Rinse and shred. Mix all ingredients with chicken.

COOKING: Steam for 12 minutes stirring occasionally. Serve immediately. *Serves 4.*

Steamed Three Variety Eggs [SAM WONG DUN]

2 *eggs*	1 *teaspoon sherry*
½ *cup water*	½ *teaspoon vegetable oil*
1 *salted duck's egg*	1 *hundred-year-old egg*
¼ *teaspoon sugar*	

PREPARATION: Use ½ cup of lukewarm water that has been boiled for at least 5 minutes and cooled. Break 2 eggs into dish. Add white of duck's egg. Take yolk and chop very fine. Add this to eggs. Add boiled water, sugar, sherry, and oil. Mix together, being careful not to overbeat. Wash and peel hundred-year-old egg. Cut into quarters and place in egg mixture as attractively as possible.

COOKING: Steam for about 10 minutes. Dish is done when consistency is like custard and no longer runny. *Serves 2.*

Steamed Eggs [JING DUN]

1 cup water
2 eggs
2 teaspoons sherry
¼ teaspoon salt

Dash pepper
½ teaspoon vegetable oil
¼ teaspoon sugar

PREPARATION: Use one cup of lukewarm water that has been boiled for at least 5 minutes and cooled. This is done to insure a smooth custard-like texture to the dish. Beat eggs lightly and stir in all other ingredients, being careful not to overbeat. Again this keeps down the air content so that the dish will be smooth.

COOKING: Steam for about 10 minutes. Test with fork or toothpick. It is done when consistency is no longer runny. Serve immediately. This dish is usually served with about 1 tablespoon of soy sauce poured over the top. *Serves 2.*

This is a delicate dish that is wonderful to serve to people convalescing from stomach ailments. If used for this purpose, exclude pepper and soy sauce.

This basic recipe may be varied by adding scallions, diced roast pork, oysters, or sausages to the eggs.

Steamed Fish [JING YU]

2 generous teaspoons brown
  bean sauce
1 stalk scallion
2 thin slices ginger
1 pound butterfish, porgy, or
  sea bass

2 teaspoons sherry
¼ cup chicken stock or water
½ teaspoon sugar
Dash pepper
1 teaspoon dark soy sauce
1 tablespoon vegetable oil

PREPARATION: Mash brown beans into a brown paste. Mince scallions. Shred ginger. Slash fish diagonally on both sides and place on dish. Mix all ingredients and sprinkle over fish.

COOKING: Steam for 6 minutes. Fish is done when it flakes. *Serves 2 or 3.*

For a variation try adding 2 bean curds cut up into 8 blocks.

Steamed Fish Slices [JING YU PEEN]

1 ounce Chinese mushrooms	1 teaspoon salt
(about 5)	1 tablespoon vinegar
1 stalk scallion	1 tablespoon dark soy sauce
2–3 slices ginger	1 tablespoon vegetable oil
⅛ pound ham	¼ teaspoon sugar
1 pound sole or turbot	Generous dash pepper

PREPARATION: Soak mushrooms in cold water until soft (about 15 minutes). Wash scallion and ginger. Shred all three ingredients. Shred ham. Wash fish and cut into large slices. Rub fish thoroughly with salt. Place slices on plate with skin side down. Combine all other ingredients and cover slices with mixture.

COOKING: Steam for 6 minutes. Serve immediately. *Serves 2 or 3.*

Fresh mushrooms may be used instead of dried mushrooms. I would double the quantity.

A whole porgy or sea bass weighing 1 pound may be used instead of the slices.

Steamed Sea Bass with Mushrooms [JING YU]

2 pounds sea bass
1½ teaspoons salt
2 ounces Chinese mushrooms
  (about 10)
1 ball salted turnip
8 thin slices ginger (about 2
  tablespoons)
2 stalks scallions

Sauce for fish:
1 tablespoon vegetable oil
2 teaspoons light soy sauce
Generous dash pepper
¼ teaspoon sugar

PREPARATION: Take clean sea bass and rub once thoroughly, inside and out, with salt. Slash diagonally on both sides. Place on dish. Soak mushrooms in cold water until soft (about 15 minutes). Rinse and shred. Wash turnip and shred. Shred ginger. Mince scallions. Mix together and stuff fish with these ingredients and also place over entire exposed side of fish. Mix sauce and sprinkle over entire fish.

COOKING: Steam for 15 minutes. Fish is done when meat flakes and eyes bulge. Serve immediately. *Serves 3.*

This is my own recipe which never fails to win compliments when it is served to guests.

Steamed Lobster [JING LUNG HAR]

1 lobster
¼ pound melted butter

PREPARATION: Have butcher cut lobster into 10 pieces. Reassemble on plate.

COOKING: Steam for 4 minutes or until lobster is bright red. Pour melted butter over dish and serve immediately.

This is a far better way of cooking lobster than placing it in boiling water. In this way *all* flavors are preserved.

Steamed Lobster with Salted Egg [YOUNG LUNG HAR]

1¼ pounds lobster (1)   ½ teaspoon sugar
1 ounce Chinese mushrooms   1 teaspoon sherry
   (about 4)   1 tablespoon vegetable oil
4 water chestnuts   Dash pepper
¼ pound lean ground pork   1 salted duck's egg

PREPARATION: Cut lobster spinally in 10 pieces. Reassemble on dish. Meanwhile soak mushrooms in cold water until soft (about 15 minutes). Mince water chestnuts and mushrooms very finely. Stir into pork along with other seasonings and white of salted duck's egg. Spread pork mixture over top of lobster using fork, break egg yolk (which is quite firm), and smear over top of pork mixture.

COOKING: Steam for 20 minutes. Serve immediately. *Serves 2 to 3.*

At my husband's former restaurant the chefs would reassemble the lobster, including the head and feelers. After spreading the pork on, some chefs would use the yolk of the duck's egg to write the Chinese symbol for good health. Quite dramatic!

Steamed Sponge Cake

4 eggs   ½ teaspoon vanilla
1 cup granulated sugar   ½ teaspoon almond or lemon
1 cup self-rising flour or   extract
   1 cup flour and ½ teaspoon
   baking powder

PREPARATION: Beat egg whites until fairly stiff, then gradually add sugar. Continue beating until egg whites form stiff peaks.

Add yolks of eggs and beat for another 3 minutes at medium speed of electric mixer. Fold flour into mixture and add extract.

COOKING: Place batter in lightly greased pan and steam for 25 minutes. Cake will spring back when touched. *Serves 6.*

This cake is excellent, although not quite Chinese, as a strawberry shortcake with whipped cream and strawberries. As a typically Chinese dessert it is served plain, cut up into 2-inch squares.

MASTERING THE METHOD

OF RED COOKING

Red cooking, or cooking in soy sauce, is so called because food cooked this way turns a rich reddish-brown color. There are actually two methods of cooking that fall under this heading: *lo suey*, which is stewing in soy sauce, and *hoong siu*. Hoong siu is actually a two-step process in which the food is first deep fried, then braised in stock. Either soy or oyster sauce is used as the principal flavorer.

The stewing method is used often by the Chinese housewife. One of its advantages for her is that it is slow cooking and therefore doesn't require constant attention. Also food cooked this way keeps very well and can be served hot or cold, it can be prepared ahead of time, and it may also be "stretched" by adding vegetables for a later meal.

Lo suey is not done by restaurants because of the tremendous shrinkage of the food and also the length of time involved to prepare a dish. It would be most uneconomical for a business. For dinner parties of ten or more people, I always include at least one red-cooked meat dish in my menu. It can be prepared a day in advance.

For red stewing, a special Lee secret is to combine both light and dark soy sauce. The dark soy gives the dish its rich color and the light soy imparts its own delicate flavor.

The imported sauces are essential for this method of cooking because of the large quantities involved. The domestic type of soy would be too overpowering if used in such quantities.

Hoong siu dishes are available in most restaurants, and the results are worth the effort in the home. The deep frying adds just one more dimension in texture and taste as the food is being prepared.

Red-Cooked Winter Melon [HOONG SIU DUNG QUAR]

1 pound winter melon	½ teaspoon salt
3 cups vegetable oil	Dash pepper
1 ounce Chinese mushrooms	½ teaspoon sugar
2 teaspoons cornstarch mixed	2 tablespoons oyster sauce
with 2 teaspoons water	½ cup chicken stock or water
¼ teaspoon monosodium	
glutamate	

PREPARATION: Wash, peel, and seed melon. Cut in half. Heat oil to 375 degrees Deep fry melon until brown. Remove to paper towel. Meanwhile soak mushrooms in cold water until soft (about 15 minutes). Rinse and cut in halves. After melon cools, cut into ¾ inch wedges. Mix cornstarch, water, monosodium, salt, pepper, and sugar. Set beside pan.

COOKING: Bring soup stock to boil and add melon and mushrooms. Simmer for 10 minutes. Add oyster sauce. Remove melon and mushrooms to serving dish. Bring flame to high and thicken with cornstarch solution. Pour over melon and serve. Serves 2 or 3.

This dish is often garnished with shredded Smithfield ham or boiled ham. Also, I like to add a few leaves of parsley for color.

Red-Cooked Bean Curd [HOONG SIU DOW FU]

4 bean curd cakes	2 teaspoons sherry
2 stalks scallions	½ teaspoon sugar
2 teaspoons cornstarch mixed	1 cup chicken stock or water
with 2 teaspoons water	1 thin slice ginger
Dash pepper	2 tablespoons dark soy sauce

PREPARATION: Heat oil to 375 degrees and deep fry bean cakes until golden brown. Remove to paper towel. Mince scallions. Mix cornstarch, water, pepper, sherry, sugar, and set beside pan. Cut bean curd into 1-inch squares.

COOKING: Bring stock to boil and add ginger, bean curd, and soy sauce. Cover and lower flame and simmer for 5 minutes. Add scallions. Thicken with cornstarch mixture. *Serves 3.*

Red-Cooked Bean Curd—Variation II with Oyster Sauce [HO YAU DOW FU]

1 cup vegetable oil	Dash pepper
4 bean curd cakes	½ teaspoon sugar
1 clove garlic	1 tablespoon vegetable oil
2 stalks scallions	1 cup chicken stock or water
1 tablespoon brown bean sauce	1 tablespoon oyster sauce
2 teaspoons cornstarch mixed with 2 teaspoons water	

PREPARATION: Heat 1 cup of oil to 375 degrees and deep fry bean cakes until golden brown. Remove cakes to paper towel. Mince garlic very fine. Mince scallions. Mash brown beans. Mix cornstarch solution, pepper, sugar, and set beside pan. Cut cooled bean cakes into 1-inch squares.

COOKING: Heat pan and add 1 tablespoon of vegetable oil, garlic, and brown beans. Add cubes of bean cakes and stock. Bring to boil. Lower flame and simmer for 5 minutes. Turn flame to high. Add oyster sauce and scallions. Thicken with cornstarch mixture. *Serves 3.*

Red-Cooked Beef [LO SUEY NGOW YUK]

1 *clove garlic*	2 *cups light soy sauce*
1 *wedge ginger size of 50-cent*	2 *cups dark soy sauce*
piece	6 *cups water*
5 *pounds eye round of beef*	8 *tablespoons sugar*
10 *grains anise pepper*	*or to taste*
(optional)	2 *tablespoons sherry*
1 *star anise*	

PREPARATION: Give garlic a light tap so it is bruised and not whole. Smash wedge of ginger.

COOKING: Sear beef. This is done to seal in juices. Bring to boil other ingredients. Add beef and simmer for 1 hour and 15 minutes or until tender. Chopstick will pierce easily. Serve meat sliced hot or cold with sauce that it cooked in. The sauce, if refrigerated, may be used for a number of dishes. Chuck roast, brisket of beef, or rump roast may be used. Cooking times will vary with cuts of meat. Sometimes vegetables are added the last half hour or so. In this case the vegetable would be cut using the rolling diagonal method. You may use turnips, carrots, bamboo shoots, or even lily flowers. *Serves 6.*

This dish is often accompanied by red-cooked eggs (see page 119).

Red-Cooked Leg of Lamb [LO SUEY YANG YUK]

1 5-pound leg of lamb
2 stalks scallions

PREPARATION: Use red-cooked chicken sauce (see page 119) and add 2 stalks scallions. Cut scallions in 1-inch slices.

COOKING: Sear or brown lamb in heavy skillet. Meanwhile bring sauce to boil. Add scallions and leg of lamb. Turn flame to low. Simmer, basting and turning occasionally, for 2 hours or until meat is tender. Remove from sauce. Slice and serve with or without sauce. *Serves 6.*

Red-Cooked Pork [LO SUEY GEE YUK]

1 3-pound pork butt

PREPARATION: Use red-cooked beef sauce (see page 117).

COOKING: Bring to boil enough water to cover pork butt. Place pork in water and boil for 5 minutes. Drain and run under cold water. This is to remove excess fat, etc. Bring beef sauce to boil and place butt in sauce. Simmer for 2 hours or until very tender. Serve sliced with sauce. You may use fresh ham for this recipe. The ham will be heavier so cooking time must be increased. *Serves 4.*

Red-Cooked Chicken [SEE AU GAI]

1 whole chicken
  (5–6 pounds)
1 wedge ginger size of 50-cent
  piece
1 clove garlic
4 tablespoons sugar
  or to taste

1 star anise
2 teaspoons sherry
1 cup light soy sauce
1 cup dark soy sauce
1 cup water

PREPARATION: Wash chicken thoroughly and dry with paper towels. Some people hang chicken up a few hours before cooking. This insures greater absorption of sauce and therefore a darker, more appealing color. Smash wedge of ginger and bruise garlic. Mix all ingredients together.

COOKING: Bring combined ingredients to boil and add whole chicken. Simmer for 20 minutes on each side (total of 1 hour and 20 minutes), basting often. Remove and cool. Chop chicken into bite-size pieces and serve. Heat sauce and pour ¼ cup over chicken. *Serves 5 to 6.*

The whole chicken that Chinese use is usually a pullet of about 5 or 6 pounds. The pullet is a special type (preferably one that hasn't laid an egg) that has been kept in tiny cages and fattened. These chickens are tender and plump and have ample breast meat.

Red-Cooked Eggs [LO SUEY DUN]

1 dozen eggs

Hard cook eggs and rinse with cold water. Peel and leave soaking overnight in beef solution (see previous recipe). The eggs are really perfect if the exterior of the yolk is hard cooked and the interior is still soft. If you are really in a rush you may simmer peeled eggs for 20 minutes in beef solution, but they will not be brown throughout.

I serve red-cooked beef at large informal buffets. I usually slice it and serve it on a bed of lettuce and surround the slices with quartered red-cooked eggs. I use silver platters and try also to have slices of tomato or love apples along with it. The color combinations are quite pleasing.

Red-Cooked Chicken Livers [SEE AU GAI GONE]

½ pound chicken livers

Simmer until done in red cooked chicken sauce (see page 119). May be served cut into cubes as an hors d'oeuvre or as a side dish at the table.

For a western twist chop livers and make a pâté! Serve with crackers.

Red-Cooked Chicken Wings [SEE AU GAI YICK]

3 pounds chicken wings

Singe pin feathers off. Simmer in red-cooked chicken sauce (see page 119), until tender—about 20 minutes. Makes a wonderful snack or picnic lunch.

The sauce may be refrigerated in a tightly covered jar and used for other dishes.

Fried Fish in Vegetables [HOONG SIU YU]

1 beaten egg
5 tablespoons flour
1 pound sea bass
3 cups vegetable oil
8 Chinese mushrooms
1 tablespoon lily flowers
2 ounces pork
1 cup Chinese cabbage
3 tablespoons bamboo shoots
2 thin slices ginger
2 teaspoons cornstarch mixed
   with 2 teaspoons water

1 teaspoon sugar
½ teaspoon monosodium
   glutamate
1 teaspoon dark soy sauce
2 teaspoons sherry
Dash pepper
2 tablespoons vegetable oil
1 teaspoon salt
1½ cups chicken stock or
   water

PREPARATION: Mix batter of beaten egg and flour. Dip fish in batter. You may want to slash fish on both sides to insure faster cooking. In that case slash once diagonally on each side. Deep fry in 3 cups of oil that has been heated to 375 degrees. Fry 4 minutes on each side until fish is crisp and brown. Soak mushrooms and lily flowers in cold water for 15 minutes or until soft. Shred mushrooms, pork, Chinese cabbage, and bamboo shoots. Wash and shred ginger. Mix cornstarch solution and add sugar, monosodium, soy, sherry, and pepper. Set beside pan.

COOKING: Using a high flame, heat pan and add 2 tablespoons oil, salt, and ginger. Add pork and stir for 1½ minutes or until cooked (it will turn white). Add Chinese cabbage, mushrooms, bamboo shoots, lily flowers, and stir. Next add stock and cover for 2 minutes. Thicken with cornstarch mixture. Place fish on platter and pour vegetables over the fish. *Serves 2 to 3.*

The Chinese believe in leaving fish entirely intact with head. This insures that juices will not be lost, also some feel that the meat in the cheek is the sweetest on the whole fish. To the Chinese there is nothing more attractive than the whole fish on a platter, but to some Westerners the eyes of the fish are quite repulsive. If you share this feeling, by all means remove the head.

NOODLES

A good friend of mine once observed that a fundamental difference between the outlook of the Westerner and that of the Chinese is that, while each is convinced that his culture is the greatest, the Westerner feels that the world will be deprived if it does not learn about his, but the Chinese considers the world incapable of appreciating his culture and is therefore satisfied to keep it to himself. This may account for one reason why China's greatest art, porcelain, deteriorated so when she started to export to other parts of the world. She began to make things she considered the market capable of appreciating and the nauseating *chinoiserie* porcelain was the result. This may also account for some of the food that is served in Chinese restaurants of today, as well as the reticence of waiters who are afraid to suggest anything for fear that the diner may not enjoy it. Their idea of the Western palate is one that is rather pedestrian and fears and avoids anything exotic.

It is probably for both these reasons that the Westerner is so totally ignorant of one facet of the Chinese cuisine which he would enjoy most, and that is noodles. My husband often teasingly insists that all things originated in China. Well, I'm not so sure about "all things," but brace yourself—noodles did originate in China and not in Italy. They were in fact brought over to Italy by Marco Polo after his visit to the then distant and exotic land of Cathay. If you think there are innumerable kinds of pasta, wait until you start to explore the Chinese counterpart.

Although for the Cantonese, noodles are more a lunch and refreshment dish, people who were born and reared in the northern parts of China grew up mainly on noodles or wheat products. Between the various schools of cooking there are innumerable ways of making noodles, just as there are many kinds of noodles.

In the Chinatowns of the United States, especially New York and San Francisco, there are little tiny "noodle houses" whose specialties are noodles and then more noodles—noodles in any shape and in every way one can imagine. These houses cater mainly to Chinese trade and are the last bastions that remain relatively unexplored or untouched by Westerners.

Here on the next few pages I have chosen a few recipes which I think are outstanding, and which will surely present ways of preparing noodles very different from any you have previously tried.

Three-Flavored Noodles [SAM JUP MEIN]

½ pound noodles
½ large Spanish onion
⅛ pound roast pork
1 large tomato
½ cup catsup
½ teaspoon salt
½ teaspoon sugar

Dash pepper
1 teaspoon hoisin sauce
 (optional)
1 teaspoon monosodium
 glutamate
3 tablespoons curry powder
⅓ cup chicken stock or water

PREPARATION: Boil or steam noodles *al dente*. Rinse in cold water, and then hot water, drain, and set aside on serving dish. Slice onion into thin half rings. Shred pork. Cut tomato into wedges. Mix catsup with salt, sugar, pepper, hoisin, and monosodium. Set beside pan.

COOKING: Using a very low flame, pan fry curry powder in dry frying pan. Stir constantly for 45 seconds then add onion. Stir until curry becomes slightly brown and pungent. Add roast pork and soup stock and turn flame to high. Stir and bring to boil. Add catsup mixture and stir. At last moment add wedges of tomato. Pour sauce over noodles, arranging tomato wedges decoratively, or stir noodles in at last minute. *Serve 2 or 3.*

This is one noodle dish that is a must.

If you like your onions well done, parboil them for ½ minute or so. You may substitute cooked pork for roast pork.

Roast Pork Soft Fried Noodles [CHA SHEW LO MEIN]

¼ *pound egg noodles*
¼ *pound roast pork (see page 155)*
½ *cup Chinese cabbage*
⅔ *cup bean sprouts*
2 *tablespoons oyster sauce (or dark soy sauce)*
¼ *teaspoon sugar*

½ *teaspoon monosodium glutamate*
Liberal dash pepper
1 *tablespoon vegetable oil*
½ *teaspoon salt*
2 *tablespoons chicken stock or water*
2 *teaspoons sherry*

PREPARATION: Boil or steam noodles *al dente.* Rinse in cold water and drain. Shred pork and cabbage. Wash bean sprouts and, if desired, remove tails. Mix oyster sauce with sugar, monosodium, and pepper, and set beside pan.

COOKING: Using a high flame, heat pan and add oil and salt. Next add pork and sherry. Add vegetables and stir for 45 seconds. Next add stock and place noodles on top. Cover for 1 minute. Uncover and stir. Next add oyster sauce mixture and stir until evenly seasoned. *Serves 2.*

For variations of this recipe, you substitute shredded cooked chicken, duck, ham, or ¼ pound cooked shrimp for the pork. This dish is especially attractive if served on a large platter and garnished with minced scallion and Chinese parsley leaves.

Soft Fried Spaghetti

½ pound or box thin spa-
ghetti
¾ cup celery
¼ pound cooked meat or 2
eggs (beaten, fried, and
shredded
¼ head iceberg lettuce
1 tomato
2 stalks scallions
3 tablespoons dark soy sauce
(or oyster sauce)

Liberal dash pepper
¼ teaspoon sugar
1 tablespoon vegetable oil
½ teaspoon salt
¼ cup sliced mushrooms
2 tablespoons chicken stock
or water
2 teaspoons sherry

PREPARATION: Boil spaghetti until *al dente*. Rinse in cold water and drain. Shred celery, meat, and lettuce. Dice tomato.
Mince scallions. Mix soy with pepper and sugar and set beside pan.

COOKING: Using a high flame, heat pan and add oil and salt.
Next add celery, mushrooms, and stock. Cover for 2 minutes.
Next add meat, lettuce, and sherry. Place spaghetti on top
and cover for 45 seconds. Uncover, stir thoroughly. Add soy
mixture and stir. Just before turning flame off, stir in scallions
and tomato. *Serves 2 or 3.*

This is my own recipe. I had unexpected company one evening just before doing my weekly marketing. The refrigerator
was practically bare. So I threw together everything that was
left in it and this was the result.

Cantonese Soft Fried Chow Mein [KWANGTUNG CHOW MEIN]

1 pound egg noodles
3 tablespoons vegetable oil
2 ounces Chinese mushrooms
  (about 8–10)
½ pound roast pork or raw
  lean pork
½ cup bamboo shoots
½ cup celery
1 cup Chinese cabbage
6 snow peas
½ cup bean sprouts
  (optional)
¼ cup water chestnuts
2 stalks scallions (optional)
Enough Chinese parsley to
  garnish dish

1 clove garlic
1 tablespoon cornstarch mixed
  with 1 tablespoon water
3 tablespoons dark soy sauce
½ teaspoon sugar
1 teaspoon monosodium
  glutamate
Liberal dash pepper
½ teaspoon sesame oil
  (optional)
1 teaspoon salt
2 thin slices ginger
1 tablespoon sherry
1 cup chicken stock or water

PREPARATION: Boil or steam egg noodles until almost done. Remove and rinse with cold water. Drain. Divide into two batches. Using a high flame, heat pan and add 1 tablespoon of vegetable oil. When pan is hot, fry half batch noodles until they become slightly crisp and brown on both sides. Repeat procedure with other half (this is to give more texture to the dish. This step may be left out). Remove to large serving dish. Meanwhile soak mushrooms in cold water until soft (about 15 minutes or so). Rinse and shred. Shred pork, bamboo shoots, celery, Chinese cabbage, and cut snow peas diagonally into about ½ inch-size pieces. Wash bean sprouts and remove tails. Slice water chestnuts very thin. Mince scallions. Wash parsley and pick off leaves. Mince garlic. Mix cornstarch solution and add soy, sugar, monosodium, pepper, and sesame oil. Set beside pan.

COOKING: Using a high flame, heat pan and add remaining oil, salt, garlic, and ginger. Add pork and if raw stir for 2 minutes. (If roast pork is used, just stir and add next ingredients.) Add sherry. Next add bamboo shoots, bean sprouts, celery, Chinese cabbage, water chestnuts, and Chinese mushrooms. Add stock and cover. Cook for 3 minutes. Uncover and stir for 30 seconds. Next add snow peas. Thicken gravy with cornstarch solution. When gravy thickens stir in scallions. Add sesame oil, if desired. Remove from flame and pour over noodles in platter. Garnish with Chinese parsley leaves. *Serves 4 or 5.*

This is the de luxe version of soft fried noodles. Variations of this dish are made by substituting beef, chicken, crab meat, duck, lamb, lobster, or shrimp for the pork.

Noodles with Lobster [LUNG HAR CHOW MEIN]

½ pound egg noodles
3 tablespoons vegetable oil
½ Spanish onion
1 cup cooked lobster meat
¼ cup bamboo shoots
½ cup bean sprouts
2 teaspoons cornstarch mixed with 1 tablespoon water
2 teaspoons dark soy sauce

½ teaspoon sugar
Dash pepper
½ teaspoon monosodium glutamate
½ teaspoon salt
1 thin slice ginger
¼ cup sliced mushrooms
2 teaspoons sherry
½ cup chicken stock or water

PREPARATION: Boil noodles until cooked but very firm. Rinse in cold water. Drain. Using a high flame, heat pan and add 2 tablespoons of oil. Brown noodles on both sides. Remove to heated platter. Cut onion into thin rings, slice lobster and bamboo shoots. Wash bean sprouts and remove tails. Mix cornstarch and water, soy, sugar, pepper, and monosodium. Set beside pan.

COOKING: Using a high flame, heat pan and add 1 tablespoon of oil, salt, and ginger. Add onion and stir for 1 minute. Next add other vegetables, lobster, mushrooms, sherry, and stock. Cover for 1 minute. Uncover, stir, and thicken gravy with cornstarch mixture. Pour over top of noodles. *Serves 2 or 3.*

Brown Bean Sauce Noodles [JAR CHIANG MEIN]

4–5 Chinese mushrooms
1 clove garlic
1½ pound egg noodles
4 tablespoons yellow or brown bean sauce
1 tablespoon vegetable oil
½ teaspoon salt

1 pound ground pork (or beef)
2 tablespoons hoisin sauce
½ cup chicken stock or water
¼ teaspoon cayenne pepper (optional)
½ teaspoon sugar

PREPARATION: Soak mushrooms in cold water until soft (about 15 minutes). Rinse and dice. Mince garlic. Boil noodles *al dente* (firm). Rinse in cold water. Mash brown beans.

COOKING: Using a high flame, heat pan and add oil, salt, and garlic. Next add pork and mushrooms and stir. Add sauces and stock. Cover and cook on medium flame for 5 minutes, stirring often. Add cayenne pepper and sugar. Rinse noodles in hot water to heat, drain. Place in serving dish and spoon sauce over noodles. *Serves 6.*

Traditionally the noodles and sauce are served separately and everyone mixes his own bowl according to taste. Along with the sauce there are other accompaniments. I usually mix everything together for an informal buffet, for example, cold shredded radishes, cold shredded cucumbers, cold shredded celery, minced scallions, garnish of Chinese parsley leaves. Here is how I fix my cucumbers and celery.

2 cups celery finely shredded
and blanched
1 cucumber finely shredded
½ teaspoon sesame oil
1 tablespoon peanut oil
½ teaspoon sugar

1 tablespoon light soy sauce
1 teaspoon monosodium
glutamate
½ teaspoon salt
Liberal dash pepper

Mix and chill.

One Order Noodles in Soup [YAT GAW MEIN]

½ pound egg noodles
¼ pound roast pork
1 stalk scallion
1 can chicken broth or 2 cups
homemade stock

1 cup sliced Chinese cabbage
Few sprigs Chinese parsley

PREPARATION: Boil or steam noodles until soft. Shred roast pork. Mince scallion.

COOKING: Open can of broth and follow directions in diluting. Bring to boil and add Chinese cabbage. Cook cabbage until done to your taste. Meanwhile place noodles in deep bowls. Spread shredded pork over top. Next pour stock and Chinese cabbage over noodles. Garnish with scallion and Chinese parsley leaves. Serve with light soy sauce so that diner may season soup to suit his taste. *Serves 2.*

This is an excellent simple lunch or snack. Instead of roast pork you may substitute ham or chicken. I have also used fried Polish sausage (which has been shredded) or canned Spam. If you can't get Chinese cabbage use lettuce which has been shredded. I have often used packaged spaghetti instead of the traditional Chinese noodles.

Yang Chow Noodles in Soup De Luxe [YANG CHOW WO MEIN]

½ pound egg noodles
½ ounce Chinese mushrooms
 (2 or 3)
1 cup sliced Chinese cabbage
¼ cup bamboo shoots
⅛ pound roast pork
4 water chestnuts
3 snow peas
1 ounce cooked chicken

1 ounce cooked roast duck
1 ounce fried fish maw
1 ounce cooked chicken or
 pork liver
1 ounce cooked shrimp
Few ham slices
1 can chicken broth or
 2 cups homemade stock

PREPARATION: Boil or steam egg noodles until soft (about 7 minutes if fresh egg noodles are used), rinse with cold water, and drain. Place in deep soup tureen. Meanwhile soak mushrooms in cold water until soft. Wash Chinese cabbage and slice. Slice bamboo shoots, pork, water chestnuts, and divide snow peas into halves or thirds according to size. All cooked meats and fish should be cut into uniform slices.

COOKING: Open can of broth and follow instructions in diluting. Bring to boil and add cabbage, bamboo shoots, water chestnuts, and mushrooms. Cook cabbage to desired consistency (about 2 minutes for me). Add snow peas at the end. Arrange cooked meats and fish on top of noodles in tureen. (You may pass them through hot stock to get them warm if they are cold.) Pour stock and vegetables over noodles and meats and fish. *Serves 2 or 3.*

This dish is really served only in restaurants, as it calls for so many cooked ingredients in such small quantities that it would actually be impractical for the home. However, it might give you some ideas on how to use your leftovers at home.

Noodles in Soup with Pickled Mustard Green [YTS YOW TZU MEE]

6 tablespoons pickled cabbage (about ⅓ pound) (see page 20)

⅛ pound roast pork or ⅛ pound pork that has been cooked or ⅛ pound cooked shrimp

½ pound egg noodles
1 can chicken stock or 2 cups homemade stock

PREPARATION: Wash pickled cabbage, drain water thoroughly, and shred. Shred pork, boil noodles until soft.

COOKING: Prepare stock according to directions and bring to boil. Place cabbage, shrimp, and pork in soup and turn off flame. Pour over noodles and serve. *Serves 2 or 3.*

Cold Noodles

1 pound egg noodles

Cook until soft. Rinse in cold water and drain. Refrigerate in covered dish.

Traditionally the noodles are served separately with various things and the guest mixes his own dish, but I find that at summer dinner parties the premixed noodles can be made ahead of time and are a boon to the busy hostess. Here are different variations.

VARIATION I:

2 tablespoons vegetable oil	Liberal dash pepper
1 teaspoon sesame oil	2 stalks scallions finely minced
1 tablespoon light soy sauce	½ teaspoon sugar
1½ cups precooked bean sprouts	Salt to taste

Very bland and light and can be served instead of potato salad.

VARIATION II:

You may use ½ pound of shredded meat, such as cooked spiced beef or roast pork. Crabmeat that has been fried with ginger and seasoned with sherry, etc., is especially delicious mixed in with noodles.

This may start your mind working and I'm sure you can think of many more ways to serve noodles cold with the many different vegetables that are so easy to get in the summer.

RICE

No Chinese cookbook would be complete without a section on rice, and for a really successful Chinese dinner the rice must be cooked to a perfect consistency. Raw polished rice should be purchased; precooked varieties are never used. There are basically two types of raw polished white rice, long grain and short grain. The Chinese prefer the long-grain rice, which cooks drier and has more texture after it is cooked. The short-grain rice, used by the Japanese, requires much less water as it cooks starchier. The Texas Patna or any long-grained rice available on the shelves of the supermarket is adequate.

The pot in which you cook rice is very important and should be selected carefully. If you have a family of four to six, a two-quart saucepan with a lid that fits snugly is adequate. I always recommend heavy-gauge aluminum pots for rice. They conduct just enough heat and they conduct it evenly, so if the rice is left on low flame for longer than usual it doesn't burn but just forms a thin brown crust. Copper-bottom pots, however, will cause the rice to burn, and charred rice is very difficult to remove from the pot. In Chinese homes, if the dinner is unexpectedly delayed, the rice is kept on the very lowest flame for as long as 45 minutes after it is done. If rice is left sitting in a cold pot, it gets hard and unpalatable.

Once you have made your choice of pot, stick to it. Always cook rice in the same pot. In this way you will get to know your pot very well and be able to judge how much water to use or how much rice is enough for the number of people you are serving. As a rule 1 cup of raw rice is enough for 3 people.

The first step in preparing rice is to wash it to remove dust particles and also the coating of white rice dust that inevitably covers all the grains. If rice is washed improperly or not at all, when it is cooked it will have a chalky yellowish-white appearance due to the sediment.

The pot should never be more than half filled with raw rice. If you must cook more, use a larger pot.

The biggest question about the cooking of rice concerns the amount of water to add. This is a matter of experience. If the rice is old it will require more water. Chinese housewives have various ways of measuring. Some place their whole hand, palm down, across the washed rice and add water until it covers the top of the knuckles. Others use their fingers and add water up to the first joint of their fingers. A more accurate method might be a cup and a half of water for every cup of raw rice. I might add, though, that it really is a matter of trial and error. The desired consistency of rice varies from person to person.

The rice is started with a high flame. The pot is covered so that the boiling point will be reached sooner. When the water starts to boil, uncover the pot and wait until nearly all the water is boiled away and the rice is visible under a mass of bubbles. There should be air pockets in the rice. Cover the pot and turn the flame to simmer. Steam for fifteen minutes or so until the rice is soft and fluffy.

Roast Pork Fried Rice [CHA SHEW CHOW FUN]

3 cups cooked rice
½ cup roast pork
¼ cup onion (about ½ large onion)
¼ cup bean sprouts
1 tablespoon vegetable oil
½ teaspoon salt
1 egg
2 teaspoons sherry

¼ cup chicken stock or water
2 teaspoons dark soy sauce
Liberal dash pepper
¼ teaspoon sugar
¼ teaspoon monosodium glutamate
1 stalk scallion (optional)

PREPARATION: Use leftover or cooled rice. Dice roast pork and onion. Wash bean sprouts and remove tails if you have the patience.

COOKING: Using a high flame, heat pan and add oil and salt. Scramble egg. Next add onion, bean sprouts and pork. Add sherry and stock and cover for 45 seconds. Add rice and break up clumps. Cover for 45 seconds. Uncover, stir thoroughly. Next add soy sauce and other dry ingredients. Stir thoroughly. Serve immediately. You may add minced scallion for color. If you do use scallion, add as you turn the flame off and stir in. *Serves 2 or 3.*

The Chinese often garnish this dish with parsley leaves (Chinese parsley of course). The amount of soy sauce varies according to taste. The amount of soup stock also varies according to how moist you like fried rice.

Fried Rice with Bacon, Lettuce, Tomatoes, and Onions

3 *cups cooked rice*	2 *tablespoons chicken stock*
¼ *head of lettuce*	*or water*
1 *large onion*	2–3 *tablespoons dark soy sauce*
1 *large tomato*	*Liberal dash pepper*
¼ *pound bacon*	¼ *teaspoon monosodium*
½ *teaspoon salt*	*glutamate*
1 *tablespoon vegetable oil*	¼ *teaspoon sugar*
2 *teaspoons sherry*	

PREPARATION: Use 3 cups leftover or cooled rice. Dice vegetables. Fry bacon for 2 minutes. Remove and slice into ¾ inch squares (divide 1 strip into about 6 pieces).

COOKING: Using a high flame, add salt and oil. Next add onion and bacon. Add sherry and stock and place rice on top. Cover for 45 seconds (this is done to soften and heat rice). Uncover and break up clumps of rice. Add lettuce and stir thoroughly. Next add soy sauce, tomato, and dry ingredients. Stir and serve. *Serves 2 or 3.*

Fried rice is basically a leftover dish. One may use practically anything in it. I often use a stalk of celery, ½ of a green pepper, leftover chicken, or ham. In this above dish I sometimes use Chinese mushrooms and a scrambled egg. Just follow the general order of cooking and your dish is sure to come out. That is, first start off with leftover rice and cooked meat. Cook your vegetables three quarters of the way before adding rice. This dish is very attractive if served on a large platter and garnished with Chinese parsley.

Beef Cooked in Rice [NGOW YUK FUN]

1 *cup raw rice*	1 *teaspoon light soy sauce*
2 *cups water*	¼ *teaspoon sugar*
1 *ball salted turnip*	*Liberal dash pepper*
(optional)	1 *teaspoon vegetable oil*
2 *slices ginger*	½ *pound ground beef*
2 *teaspoons sherry*	

PREPARATION: Wash rice and start to cook. Wash turnip and shred. Shred ginger. Mix seasonings with meat.

COOKING: After rice is done, place seasoned meat on top and simmer for 2 minutes. Stir and serve. *Serves 3.*

The Chinese cook rice much starchier for this type of dish. The recipe given above is especially good for infants starting on table food, as it is easy to eat and tasty. In this type of dish every grain of rice is saturated with the flavor of the meat used. For my infant I usually puréed carrots and celery in the blender and added them to the rice after the water boiled off. Not very Chinese but very nourishing.

Yang Chow Fried Rice [YANG CHOW CHOW FUN]

¼ cup shrimp
1 stalk scallion
¼ cup diced roast pork
Wedge iceberg lettuce (about ⅓ small head)
⅛ cup diced Smithfield or boiled ham
3 cups cooked rice
1 tablespoon vegetable oil

½ teaspoon salt
1 egg
2 teaspoons sherry
¼ cup chicken stock or water
Dash white pepper
¼ teaspoon sugar
¼ teaspoon monosodium glutamate

PREPARATION: Preboil shrimp (preferably tiny ones). Mince scallion. Dice pork, lettuce, and ham. Use leftover or cooled rice.

COOKING: Using a high flame, heat pan and add oil and salt. Scramble egg. Add pork, shrimp, ham, sherry, and stock. Next add scallion and lettuce. Place rice on top and cover for 45 seconds. Uncover and stir thoroughly, breaking up clumps of rice, if any. Add dry seasonings, stir, and serve. *Serves 2 or 3.*

This dish is named after the province of its origin and is more or less the fried rice de luxe. It is usually the last course at any formal Chinese banquet. It is always very welcome and refreshing after one has partaken of rich food beforehand, probably because it is so delicate (notice no soy is used).

Chicken Cooked in Rice [GAI FUN]

½ broiler boned chicken
1 tablespoon vegetable oil
2 tablespoons dark soy sauce
2 teaspoons sherry
2 slices ginger
½ clove garlic
½ teaspoon pepper

½ teaspoon sugar
1 ounce Chinese mushrooms (about 5)
½ ball salted turnip (optional)
3 cups water
1½ cups raw rice

PREPARATION: Dice chicken. Marinate in vegetable oil, soy, sherry, ginger, minced garlic, pepper, and sugar. Soak mushrooms in cold water until soft. Rinse and dice. Wash turnip and dice. Mix both ingredients into chicken. Wash rice and add water.

COOKING: After water of rice has boiled away, place chicken on top of rice and lower flame. Simmer until rice and chicken are cooked, about 25 minutes. Stir thoroughly and serve hot. *Serves 4.*

In both recipes chicken broth may be substituted for half the amount of required water.

Minced Clams in Rice

1 *cup raw rice*	2 *teaspoons sherry*
2 *1½-ounce cans minced*	½ *teaspoon sugar*
clams	2 *teaspoons soy sauce*
Enough water with clam juice	2 *thin slices ginger*
to make 2 cups	*Dash pepper*

PREPARATION: Wash rice. Open cans of clams and pour off juice. Add enough water to make 2 cups.

COOKING: Add this to rice and start to cook. Add seasonings to clams. When rice is done, stir in clams and cover for 2 minutes. Serve immediately. *Serves 3.*

This is my own invention. My son adored it when he started table food and still enjoys it now.

Basic Congee [JOOK]

¼ *cup raw rice*
2 *quarts water*
2 *salted duck's eggs or*
   ⅛ *pound dried scallops or*
   1 *tablespoon dried shrimp*
½ *tangerine peel (optional)*

Wash rice. Add water and washed duck's eggs (or scallops or shrimps) and tangerine peel. Bring to boil. Simmer for 2½ hours or more. *Serves 4.*

Congee is a rice gruel which the Chinese are very fond of. They usually have it as a snack at any hour of the day. Very often if there is anyone ill in the household you will find a pot of congee simmering on the stove. Because it is so bland it is wonderful for those recovering from any minor intestinal disorder. I would exclude the scallops or shrimps if used for this purpose. However, under ordinary circumstances, serve it piping hot in large bowls garnished with minced scallion and Chinese parsley leaves. I also have light soy sauce at the table for added seasoning if desired.

For variations of congee the basic gruel is made with or without the duck's eggs etc., and the other ingredients are added at the end and left simmering until done.

Beef Congee [NGOW YUK JOOK]

½ pound ground beef
1 teaspoon sherry
¼ teaspoon sugar
1 teaspoon light soy sauce
½ teaspoon vegetable oil

½ teaspoon ginger finely minced
Dash pepper
1 stalk scallion minced

Mix ingredients and add to congee. Simmer for 3 minutes. You may also stir in a beaten egg for color. *Serves 4.*

Fish Congee [YU JOOK]

½ pound fish fillet sliced
1 tablespoon vegetable oil
Liberal dash pepper
1 slice ginger shredded

1 teaspoon sherry
2 teaspoons light soy sauce
¼ teaspoon sugar
½ teaspoon salt

Mix ingredients together and arrange on platter. Slices are placed in bowls of congee at table. *Serves 4.*

For added texture try shredding lettuce and mix into congee.

Pork Chops in Jook

> 2 *lean pork chops*
> 2 *teaspoons sherry*

PREPARATION: On the night before, rub chops liberally with salt; and sprinkle 2 teaspoons sherry over chops. Let stand in refrigerator overnight.

COOKING: Simmer in congee for 40 minutes. Before serving, remove from congee and slice into bite-size squares. Serve with light soy sauce. Pieces of pork are then dipped into soy before eating. *Serves 4.*

Chicken Congee [GAI JOOK]

> ¼ *pound chicken fillet*   1 *teaspoon vegetable oil*
> 1 *teaspoon sherry*   *Liberal dash pepper*
> 1 *teaspoon light soy sauce*   ½ *teaspoon sugar*
> ½ *teaspoon salt*   2 *thin slices ginger*

Cut chicken into bite-size squares. Mix all ingredients together. Stir into congee and simmer for 8 minutes. *Serves 4.*

SOUPS

Bean Curd Soup [DOW FU TONG]

2 ounces pork
1 cup Chinese cabbage
2 tablespoons bamboo shoots
2 water chestnuts
2 bricks bean curd
1 quart chicken stock or water
1 teaspoon monosodium glutamate (if water is used)
Salt to taste (½ teaspoon or so)

¼ teaspoon sugar
Dash pepper
Few drops sesame oil (optional)

Marinade for meat:
¼ teaspoon cornstarch
⅛ teaspoon light soy sauce
Few drops vegetable oil
½ teaspoon sherry

PREPARATION: Slice pork, cabbage, bamboo shoots, and water chestnuts. Add marinade to pork. Cut bean curd into 1-inch cubes.

COOKING: Bring stock to boil. Add pork and continue cooking for 3 minutes. Next add vegetables and bean curd and cook for 3 minutes. Just before turning flame off add seasonings, including sesame oil. *Serves 4.*

Some people, to make the dish more interesting, poach an egg in the soup at the end of the cooking process.

Chinese Mustard Cabbage Soup [GUY CHOY TONG]

½ pound Chinese mustard
   cabbage
2 ounces pork or beef
1 slice ginger
1 can chicken stock or
   1 quart water
1 teaspoon monosodium
   glutamate

½ teaspoon salt or to taste
¼ teaspoon sugar

Marinade for meat:
¼ teaspoon cornstarch
⅛ teaspoon light soy sauce
Few drops vegetable oil
½ teaspoon sherry

PREPARATION: Wash and slice mustard cabbage across grain into slices about ½ to ¾ inch wide. Slice meat into thin slices. Add marinade. Wash ginger and slice off 1 very thin piece.

COOKING: Bring stock to boil and add mustard cabbage and, if pork is used, pork and ginger. Cook for 9 minutes. Just before turning off flame add seasonings. After flame is turned off, if beef is used, add beef. *Serves 4.*

Corn Soup [GAI YUNG SOOK MEI]

¼ pound boned white
   chicken meat
1 can cream-style corn
1 cup chicken stock or water
1 teaspoon cornstarch mixed
   with 1 tablespoon water

½ teaspoon salt or to taste
½ teaspoon monosodium
   glutamate
1 egg white

PREPARATION: Mince chicken finely or place in blender. Remove tendons.

COOKING: Bring mixture of corn and stock to boil and thicken with cornstarch. Add seasonings. Turn flame off and stir in chicken and beaten egg white. *Serves 4.*

Egg Drop Soup [DUN FAR TONG]

1 egg
2 drops vegetable oil
1 quart chicken stock (1 can broth)
3 tablespoons cornstarch mixed with 3 tablespoons water

¼ teaspoon monosodium glutamate
¾ teaspoon salt
¼ teaspoon sugar

PREPARATION: Beat egg and add vegetable oil. If a grade-A egg is used, thin with 1 teaspoon water.

COOKING: Bring stock to boiling point and thicken with cornstarch solution. Turn flame off and add egg very slowly, stirring constantly. (You may wish to use only half, or less, of the egg.) Add monosodium, sugar, and salt. *Serves 4.*

This is a favorite in restaurants but is rarely served in the Chinese home.

Summer Melon Soup [JEET QUAR TONG]

1 summer melon
2 ounces pork
1 quart chicken stock or water
1 teaspoon monosodium glutamate (not necessary if stock is used)
Salt to taste
½ teaspoon sugar

Marinade for pork:
¼ teaspoon cornstarch
⅛ teaspoon light soy sauce
Few drops vegetable oil
½ teaspoon sherry

PREPARATION: Peel melon. Cut in half lengthwise, then slice as you would a cucumber. Slice pork and add marinade.

COOKING: Bring stock to boil. Add melon and cook for 8 minutes. Add pork the last 4 minutes. Just before turning off flame, add seasonings. *Serves 4.*

Zucchini may be substituted for summer melon. Peel, slice, and proceed with cooking.

Sour and Hot Soup [SHUEN LOT TONG]

2 tablespoons bamboo shoots
⅛ pound pork or any leftover pork
2 bricks bean curd
2 water chestnuts
2 tablespoons mushrooms
4 cloud's ears
1 egg
1 tablespoon cornstarch mixed with ½ cup water
1 teaspoon monosodium glutamate (reduce to ½ if stock is used)

1 tablespoon light soy sauce
¼ teaspoon black pepper or tabasco to taste or
1 teaspoon hot sesame oil
1 quart water or stock (beef or chicken)
½ teaspoon salt
¼ teaspoon sugar
2 tablespoons peas
3 tablespoons vinegar

PREPARATION: Shred bamboo shoots and pork. Cut bean curd into cubes. (You may use pressed bean curd; if so, shred.) Slice water chestnuts, mushrooms, and halve cloud's ears. Beat egg. Mix cornstarch with water, monosodium, soy, and pepper if you use pepper). Set beside pan.

COOKING: Bring stock to boil. Add pork at this point if uncooked. Add vegetables. After 1 minute thicken with cornstarch solution. Turn flame down and slowly add egg, stirring constantly. Turn flame off and add vinegar (if you use Tabasco or hot sesame oil, add at this point). *Serves 6.*

This is basically a soup in which leftovers are used.

WHAT TO DRINK

Contrary to popular belief, tea is not the beverage served with a good Chinese meal. Although here in America, tea is served in Chinese-American restaurants, in China rice wine was usually served throughout the meal. Tea is served at the end of a meal, as one would serve demitasse, or between meals.

Because of the political situation there are not many Chinese rice wines available on the market and the ones that may be purchased are rather overpowering in flavor and not smooth or mellow. I find that an excellent substitute is Japanese sake heated lukewarm.

Sherry is the closest thing to Chinese rice wine and is therefore the logical substitute in cooking. But sherry throughout a meal (even the dryest sherry) may be too heavy or too sweet. It traditionally makes a good apéritif or may be served with the soup course. A good wine to serve throughout a Chinese meal would be a dry Chablis (French white burgundy) or soave Bolla (Italian white wine which is dry but lighter bodied than French wine).

In recent years, however, the word wine has been indicative only of an alcoholic beverage, for I have seen straight scotch whiskey or brandy served and called "wine," the point being that spirits help to promote the mood of a wonderful meal regardless of kind. It is purely a matter of personal taste.

If your personal taste happens to favor tea over wine, then a word on teas. Tea is the beverage of the Orient. In Japan it is called o cha, in Korea and Russia cha—all stemming from the Cantonese word for tea. The word tea itself is a corruption of *tay* a Chinese dialect word for tea.

Teas are classified internationally into three major groups, green, oolong, and black (or red in China). These groups indicate what kind of processing has been done to the actual tea leaf. In green tea, the leaves have been picked and dried as is. In black tea, the chlorophyll in the leaves has been altered by an oxidizing process which changes the natural color and alters the flavor of the leaves. In oolong, the leaves have been semi-fermented or partially oxidized.

From these three major groupings the leaves are then classified according to leaf sizes. Here some confusion is encountered, for the Chinese and English use different systems.

The Chinese system classifies leaves as Imperial, young hyson, hyson, gunpowder, and twanky. The finest leaves would be classified as Imperial or young hyson.

The English have two major classifications of tea, Broken and Leaf. Broken indicates the smaller leaves taken from a bulk of tea and Leaf is the remaining larger leaves in the same bulk. The English go one step further and classify these two groups by size and appearance of the leaves. The size classifications for leaf are flowery orange pekoe, orange pekoe, Broken pekoe Souchong, Fannings, and Dust. Generally speaking, the Broken teas are darker in color and stronger in flavor.

The Chinese tea served in restaurants is usually black (or red) tea.

After unusually rich or greasy meals I like to serve a very heavy tea called *Bow Le* which somehow cuts the heaviness and clears the palate. Bow Le is difficult to purchase in this country. Another favorite of mine after heavy meals is Darjeeling tea. This tea is a blend of Chinese and the heavier-bodied Indian tea. The finest Chinese black tea available in this country is *Keemun*. This tea is best known for its smooth flavor. Jasmine and lychee teas are a combination of blossoms and black tea. These teas are particularly refreshing between meals, perhaps with tidbits and are both available in this country.

Oolong tea has a distinctly smoky flavor and is a favorite among the Chinese.

Green tea has the finest leaves of all the teas and is supposed to have the purest flavor because nothing has been done to alter the leaves. But green tea happens also to be the most potent in flavor so smaller amounts should be used as compared to the other types of tea. The finest Chinese green tea is Dragon's Well (*Lung Jing*) and is available in this country. My one objection to some Chinese green teas is that they are improperly packaged and ferment or lose some flavor during shipping to this country.

Dragon's Well is often mixed with chrysanthemum flowers to make a divine brew that is both fragrant and smoky. This extra special tea is usually served with Chinese pastry at high tea and may be taken with rock candy. I prefer it plain. It is difficult to purchase but is available upon request in the larger restaurants in New York and San Francisco.

Reams and reams have been written on how to make a "proper" pot of tea. Each country has its own way but if you use China tea then by all means learn to make a pot the Chinese way.

Start off with an acceptable tea. Choose a China pot, as metal pots may distort the flavor of the tea. The pot should be squat and round. This allows maximum exposure of tea leaves to the water because of the larger area. The pot should be scalded.

Fill a kettle with freshly drawn water, bring the water to a rolling boil, and turn the flame off. Do not overboil as this causes loss of oxygen and the result is a flat-tasting tea. Immediately add the water to the pot which has been scalded and which contains the proper amount of tea. Allow tea to steep from three to five minutes.

The proper amount of tea is really an individual thing, but if one must err then it is better to make the tea too strong than too weak. Many people have available a pot of hot water for those who prefer their tea weaker.

Since I prefer a more delicate brew, I suggest using one heaping tablespoon of black tea for 6 cups. Green tea is stronger so a heaping teaspoon for 6 cups is adequate.

Tea should be stored in air-tight containers as exposure to air causes loss of flavor. Do not keep tea for more than 6 months; really good tea should be enjoyed and shared with others and not kept forever.

DESSERTS

If I were asked to compare the French school of cooking with the Chinese, I would have to say that the Chinese school far surpasses the French in sophistication and variety with the exception of two things. The first is egg dishes and the second is desserts. The French, I believe, are unchallenged masters in both. But if Chinese desserts have been somewhat "neglected" in Western eyes, it is because the Eastern and Western attitudes are quite different.

Dessert as defined in the dictionary is a course, usually sweet, served at the end of a meal. In China the dessert course may come between courses or at the end. Desserts are served only at banquets or on a special occasion and never after everyday meals. It is only with the gradual westernization of some Chinese that the practice has changed, especially in Chinese restaurants.

In China sweet pastries were made only on festival days. These were meant to be taken between meals with tea. The oven was nonexistent in the average Chinese household so cakes and cookies were bought from a cake shop.

I personally find most Chinese desserts too heavy and sweet, or flat, but in all fairness it really is a matter of individual taste. For this book I have specially chosen three recipes of Chinese desserts which I feel are excellent.

When a Chinese meal is served to guests in our home, the dessert is always light, usually fruit in season, a fresh fruit cup, or compote, mousse, or one of the following recipes.

Almond Cookies [HUNG YAN BENG]

3 cups flour
1 teaspoon baking powder
1 cup shortening
1½ cups sugar
1 egg

½ teaspoon vanilla extract
1 teaspoon almond extract
Blanched almonds
¼ teaspoon salt

Sift flour and baking powder and salt. Cream shortening and sugar. Beat egg. Add egg, vanilla extract, and almond extract to shortening. Mix in dry ingredients. Knead dough until firm. Roll out until about ½-inch thick and cut dough into round shapes with a cookie cutter or make balls and flatten on greased cookie sheet. Decorate with blanched almonds. Place in moderate oven (350 degrees) for 25 minutes or until brown. *Makes 60 cookies.*

Almond Junket [HUNG YAN DOW FU]

1 can fruit cocktail
3 cups water
1½ packages Knox gelatin

¼ cup sugar
½ cup evaporated milk
1 tablespoon almond extract

Chill fruit cocktail. Meanwhile heat 3 cups water and dissolve gelatin and sugar in water. Remove from flame and cool for 1 minute. Slowly stir in evaporated milk and extract. Cool and refrigerate in flat pan. Cut into diamond shape and spoon fruit cocktail over junket. A delightfully light dessert and one that I think is especially appropriate after a rich Chinese meal. For a Western twist, try a mold. *Serves 6.*

Honeyed Apples

4 *apples*	3 *cups vegetable oil*
2 *egg whites*	¼ *cup vegetable oil*
2 *tablespoons cornstarch*	½ *cup honey*
2 *tablespoons flour*	1 *tablespoon sesame seeds*

Peel and core apples. Cut into uniform wedges. Make smooth batter of egg whites, cornstarch, and flour. Coat wedges with batter and deep fry in 3 cups of oil heated to 375 degrees. Fry until apples brown. Drain. Heat ¼ cup of oil and add honey; when combined and heated, add apples and sesame seeds. Stir until apples are coated. *Serves 4.*

RECIPES USING OTHER
COOKING METHODS

Shrimp Toast [HAR TOO TZU]

1½ pounds shrimp	1 tablespoon cornstarch
1 small onion	½ teaspoon monosodium
1 slice ginger	glutamate
13 slices stale bread	2 teaspoons sherry
½ teaspoon sugar	3 tablespoons water
1 egg	Liberal dash pepper
1½ teaspoons salt	2 cups oil

PREPARATION: Wash and clean shrimp. Chop fine or use blender to chop. Chop onion and ginger very fine. Combine all ingredients and mix thoroughly. Spread on stale bread.

COOKING: Heat oil to 375 degrees and deep fry bread on shrimp side for 1½ minutes or so. Turn and brown other side of bread. Remove, place on towel to drain. Cut into four pieces and serve immediately. *Makes 52 pieces.*

A wonderful hors d'oeuvre.

Shrimp Balls [JOW HAR KOW]

2 pounds shrimp	½ teaspoon sesame oil
18 water chestnuts	1 egg white
1 tablespoon cornstarch	2 cups vegetable oil
2 tablespoons sherry	2 wedges lemon
2 teaspoons salt	
1 teaspoon monosodium	
glutamate	

PREPARATION: Clean, devein shrimp. Chop very fine, or if you have a blender chop in blender. Chop water chestnuts very fine. Mix together all ingredients except egg white and lemon.

COOKING: Heat 2 cups of oil in deep fat fryer to 375 degrees. Form mixture into balls with spoon and dip in egg white. Drop into fat. Balls will float when done. Fry a few more seconds until golden. Serve with wedges of lemon. Balls may be dipped into light soy sauce at the table. *Serves 4.*

This also makes an excellent hors d'oeuvre.

Egg Rolls [CHUEN GUEN]

1 *pound cabbage*
2 *stalks celery*
½ *pound cooked shrimp*
½ *pound cooked chicken livers*
10 *water chestnuts*
½ *pound roast pork (cha shew)*
⅓ *cup bamboo shoots*
1 *teaspoon salt*

1 *teaspoon sugar*
1 *teaspoon monosodium glutamate*
Liberal dash pepper
½ *teaspoon light soy sauce*
¼ *teaspoon sesame oil*
1 *beaten egg*
10 *egg roll skins*
3 *cups oil*

PREPARATION: Boil cabbage and celery until very tender. Drain and squeeze out excess water. Shred very fine and set aside in breezy spot to drain further. Parboil shrimp and chicken livers. Mince both. Shred water chestnuts, roast pork, and bamboo shoots. Mix all ingredients but egg together. Beat egg. Wrap filling in egg roll skins and seal with egg.

COOKING: Heat deep fat fryer to 375 degrees and drop in egg rolls. When skin turns light gold, remove from oil and drain. (At this point restaurants refrigerate them and finish the cooking process as needed.) When cool, drop again into hot oil and fry until golden brown. *Makes 10.*

The two-stage deep frying method is actually a professional

Chinese chefs' secret. It assures that the inside will be moist and not overcooked (as anything overcooked becomes dry) and the outside will be crisp.

Chinese Deep-Fried Squab [JOW BOK OPP]

2 squabs	Sea salt
2 teaspoons sherry	Lettuce
3 teaspoons dark soy sauce	3 cups oil
2 wedges lemon	

PREPARATION: Cut squabs in half lengthwise by cutting through spine. Rub with sherry and soy. Set aside.

COOKING: Heat oil to 400 degrees and deep fry squab for 1 minute. Remove and drain on paper towel. Cool. When cooled, deep fry for another minute or so until dark brown. *Serves 2.*

Again I recommend the two-stage process in deep frying. Here it is especially important for a perfect result. The squab will be crisp on the outside but still moist and tender on the inside. The professional chef who taught me this Chinese secret was a perfectionist and always prepared squab this way. Unfortunately, aside from this particular chef, I haven't found another Chinese chef who will take the time to prepare this dish correctly, and the result of this haste is a soggy mess.

The squab should be quartered before serving. The traditional way is to have sea salt (unrefined salt with a hearty flavor) at the table. The squab is placed on a bed of lettuce with wedges of lemon. Lemon juice is then squeezed liberally over the pieces and these are dipped into the sea salt and enjoyed.

If I have taken pains describing everything about this dish, it is because it happens to be one of my favorites (if prepared correctly) and I can never get enough of it.

Roast Pork [CHA SHEW]

1 or 2 pounds pork	1 tablespoon light soy sauce
1 teaspoon brown bean sauce	½ teaspoon five-flavored
1 clove garlic	spice powder
½ cup chicken stock or water	½ teaspoon tomato or red
2 tablespoons salt	food coloring
4 tablespoons sugar	1 teaspoon sherry

PREPARATION: Cut pork into rectangles approximately 6 inches by 3 inches and 1 to 1½ inches thick. Mash brown beans into paste. Mince garlic very fine. Place brown bean sauce, garlic, stock, salt, sugar, and soy into a 1-quart saucepan and heat until mixture blends. (Do not boil.) Remove from flame and add five-flavored spice powder, coloring, and sherry. Pour over pork slabs and marinate for at least 6 hours. (Preferably overnight.)

COOKING: Preheat oven to 450 degrees and place rectangular shallow pan filled with water on bottom of oven. Grease oven rack with vegetable oil. Place rack at least 7 inches above pan of water. Place pork slabs directly on rack. The pan serves two purposes: it catches drippings and keeps meat from drying out. Bake at 450 degrees for 15 minutes. Reduce heat to 350 degrees. Cook pork for 10 minutes longer. *Serves 4.*

You may use pork tenderloin, boned pork butt, fresh ham, or boned pork shoulder for this dish. Some people glaze the pork by spreading a very thin coat of honey over pork during the last 10 minutes. This may make it too sweet for your taste.

The pan of water is my own personal invention. I thought of it after seeing the large Chinese roasting ovens which the restaurants use. They make roast pork and roast whole ducks and chickens in these large chambers, which have a large pan of water on the bottom directly above the flame. This method never fails to keep whatever is being roasted juicy and succulent.

Barbecued Spare-ribs [SHEW PAI QUOT]

1 teaspoon brown bean sauce
  (optional)
4 cloves garlic
¼ cup chicken stock or water
1 sheet spare-ribs (12-16 ribs)

4 tablespoons dark soy sauce
4 tablespoons sugar or honey
3 tablespoons hoisin sauce
1 tablespoon sherry

Mash brown beans into paste. Mince garlic very fine. Mix all ingredients except ribs together. (They will mix better if you heat the stock.) Marinate ribs for at least 6 hours. Preheat oven at 375 degrees. Place ribs, still in sauce, in oven for 15 minutes. Lower temperature to 300 for 10 minutes. Remove ribs from oven. (At this point they may be cooled and refrigerated until you are ready to serve them.) Just before serving, place ribs on rack in broiler and broil until brown and crisp on both sides. (Actually only about 2 or 3 minutes.) *Serves 2.*

Serve with duck sauce.

Lion's Head [TSE JEE TAO]

1½ pounds ground pork or
  beef
6 Chinese mushrooms
4 stalks scallions
10 water chestnuts
5 cups Chinese cabbage or ¾
  pound spinach
1 tablespoon sherry
1½ teaspoons salt
1 egg
1½ teaspoons cornstarch

Dash pepper
½ teaspoon sesame oil
½ teaspoon sugar
1½ teaspoons cornstarch
  mixed with 1 tablespoon
  water
1 tablespoon vegetable oil
¾ cup chicken stock
2 slices ginger
¼ cup dark soy sauce

PREPARATION: Soak mushrooms in cold water until soft (about 15 minutes). Rinse and mince fine. Mince scallions and water chestnuts. Wash and slice cabbage (or wash spinach). Add minced water chestnuts, scallions, and mushrooms to meat. Add sherry, salt, egg, cornstarch, pepper, sesame oil, and sugar to meat. Combine well but be very careful not to overhandle meat as it tends to lose its juices if mixed too long. Shape into balls. Mix cornstarch solution.

COOKING: In deep skillet add vegetable oil and brown balls. Remove and pour off fat. Place balls back into pan and add stock, ginger, and soy. Bring to boil. Cover, lower flame, and simmer for 20 minutes. Add sliced cabbage on top of meat balls. Simmer for another 10 minutes. Remove and place cabbage on bottom of serving dish and meat balls on top of bed of cabbage. Thicken sauce with cornstarch mixture and pour over dish.

Thrice-Cooked Pork [CAW YUK]

4 cloves garlic
1 wedge ginger size of quarter
½ cup red bean curd
3 tablespoons brown sugar
½ teaspoon five-flavored spice powder
2 teaspoons red coloring (optional)
3 tablespoons light soy sauce

1 tablespoon honey
3 medium-size potatoes, or 2 taro
2 pounds belly pork (fresh bacon)
1 tablespoon vegetable oil
½ teaspoon salt
1 tablespoon sherry

PREPARATION: Mince garlic very fine. Wash ginger and smash. Mince very fine. Mix red bean curd, brown sugar, five-flavored spice powder, red coloring, soy, and honey. Set beside pan. Peel and slice potatoes or taro into pieces ¼ inch thick or thinner if possible and 1½ inches square.

COOKING:

Step I: Boil strips of belly pork for 10 minutes. Remove and cool. Cut against grain into slices approximately ¼ inch thick.

Step II: Using a high flame, heat pan and add oil, salt, ginger, and garlic. Next add pork and stir for 1 minute. Add sherry and continue stirring. Add red bean curd mixture and stir until pork is completely coated.

Step III: Arrange pork and potatoes in alternate layers on an oven-proof dish. Steam for 1 hour.

This is an excellent dish to serve to company because it doesn't require constant watching and the first two steps can be done ahead of time. I usually leave out the potatoes and steam the pork by itself. After it is done I transfer it to a heated platter and serve it with steamed buns. For buns buy any commerical brown-and-serve package and steam for 3 or 4 minutes. The piece of pork is then placed on the bun to make a delightful sandwich.

The Chinese very often poach delicate meats and fish. This method of cooking, if done correctly, points up the natural flavors of the food. The quality of whatever is being cooked must be superior.

Poached Sea Bass [BAK SUEY YU]

1 *very fresh sea bass*	3 *tablespoons vegetable oil*
Wedge ginger size of 50-cent	2 *teaspoons salt*
piece	2 *tablespoons light soy sauce*
3 *tablespoons shredded ginger*	*Liberal dash pepper*
3 *stalks scallions*	

Place enough water in the pan to cover the fish and allow it to float. Heat the water to the boiling point. Wash and smash ginger. Lower flame until water only simmers. Add ginger, then fish. Increase heat until water almost boils, then reduce to simmer and let fish poach for 7 minutes. Turn off flame and leave fish in hot water. Fish is done when eyes turn completely chalk white and look as though they are ready to fall out. Fish will also flake if tested with fork or chopstick. Meanwhile shred ginger and mince scallions. Toast shredded ginger in hot boiling oil until quite brown. Place fish on serving dish. Sprinkle salt, soy, pepper, and scallions over it. Pour boiling oil and ginger shreds over. *Serves 4.*

Poached Chicken [BAK JAM GAI]

1 6 pound pullet
Enough water to cover chicken
Wedge ginger size of 50-cent piece

Bring water to boil. Add ginger. Place chicken in pot and bring water to boil again. Immediately turn flame to low. Cover and simmer (very slowly) for 12 minutes on each side. Turn flame off and leave chicken in covered pot to cool. Remove chicken and cut into bite-size pieces. Arrange on large platter.

I might add at this point that the Chinese leave the head on the chicken so that no juices are lost.

This chicken is usually served cold with a number of sauces or salt and pepper. Here are two sauces.

Hoisin sauce with scallions cut into inch-long pieces. The diner smothers chicken with this sauce.

Another sauce would be cooked peanut oil mixed with soy sauce (light soy if you have it), shredded ginger, and scallions.

The quality of the chicken used for this dish has everything to do with its success. Therefore, I specify a pullet (preferably one that hasn't laid an egg—a young one) and one that is absolutely freshly killed. *Serves 6.*

Cold Cucumber Salad Chinese Style

3 cups shredded cucumbers
   (about 2 small cucumbers)
1 teaspoon sesame oil
1 tablespoon peanut oil
½ teaspoon sugar
1 tablespoon light soy sauce
½ teaspoon vinegar
1 teaspoon monosodium
   glutamate
2 tablespoons salt

Optional:
1 clove garlic
½ teaspoon cayenne pepper
   or to taste or ½ teaspoon
   hot sesame oil

Peel and shred cucumbers very fine. Sprinkle with salt. Let stand for 2 hours. Rinse and drain thoroughly. Mix all ingredients and chill before serving. (Garlic, if used, should be minced very fine.) *Serves 4.*

You may use celery instead of cucumber or you may combine both vegetables. If you do use celery, it should be blanched.

Cold Chicken Salad Chinese Style

2 cups leftover cooked chicken
3 cucumbers or 3 cups celery,
   shredded
1 stalk scallion
½ teaspoon ginger
5 teaspoons salad oil
1 teaspoon sesame oil
1 tablespoon vinegar
1 teaspoon sugar

3 tablespoons light soy sauce
½ teaspoon monosodium
   glutamate

Optional:
2 teaspoons hot sesame oil
   or ½ teaspoon cayenne
   pepper or tabasco sauce

Shred chicken and vegetable. (You may use a combination of celery and cucumbers.) Blanch celery. Mince scallion and chop ginger very fine. Mix in other ingredients and chill. Serve on lettuce leaves. *Serves 4.*

You may substitute a smaller amount of cooked shrimp or crabmeat (fresh or canned) for interesting variations. Turkey meat (white) may also be used.

Braised Duck with Potatoes [SHEE JAI OPP]

7-pound duck
¼ cup vegetable oil
1 tablespoon vegetable oil
4 cloves garlic
¼ cup red bean curd
2½ tablespoons brown bean sauce
1 tablespoon salt
2 leeks

¼ cup sherry
1½ quarts water
2 tablespoons sugar
2 star anise
Dash pepper
4 tablespoons light soy sauce
2 pounds potatoes
2 teaspoons cornstarch mixed with 2 tablespoons water

COOKING: Using a high flame, heat pan very hot and add ¼ cup oil. Brown whole duck in pan, turning constantly. In separate pan, after heating, add 1 tablespoon vegetable oil, garlic, red bean curd, brown bean sauce, 1 tablespoon salt. Stir until ingredients are combined. Next add leeks, sherry, water, sugar, star anise, pepper, and soy sauce. When solution has combined, fill cavity of duck with some of gravy, making sure that one of the star anise is in cavity. Truss duck. Bring remainder of mixture to boil and turn flame down after adding duck and potatoes. Simmer for 20 minutes on each side basting occasionally. When the duck is done, it is removed and cooled, then chopped into bite-size pieces. The bottom of the serving platter is lined with potatoes and the duck is placed on the top. The sauce is thickened with the cornstarch solution and poured over the top of the duck. I usually make a bed of lettuce leaves first and place everything on the lettuce. I then garnish the dish with Chinese parsley.

For cooking any whole fowl I use my 16-inch wok which is ideal for this purpose. If it is more convenient for you by all means halve the duck before cooking. Remember if you do this that it will cut down the amount of cooking time.

MENU PLANNING

In China the traditional menu for guests consisted of a wide variety of tastes and numerous dishes. Generally speaking, if unexpected guests arrived, rather than increasing the amount of a course, another dish was added to the menu. Here in America, where in most homes the hostess must double as cook, this would be hard on one's nerves and impractical if one is to have a smooth dinner party. Guests cannot possibly feel at ease if the hostess spends most of her time jumping up from the dinner table and excusing herself to run into the kitchen to prepare the next course.

The meal should always be served in the informal Chinese manner, that is, all the dishes brought to the table at once. The formal Chinese meal has each course served separately. Again, without trained help in the kitchen, this would prove rather trying for the hostess. I feel very strongly that it is important for a hostess to enjoy herself *with* her guests, so that her guests in turn will enjoy the evening.

For the novice Chinese cook, I suggest keeping the meal as simple as possible. An electric frying pan and electric deep fat fryer or dutch oven will prove indispensable, if you have a four-burner stove. If you have a six-burner stove, your prayers are answered. Regardless of the number of people one has, rice is essential and the hostess should plan on one burner being used for rice.

For four people I recommend a very simple menu (preferably one which can all be done ahead of time) consisting of rice, a meat, fowl or fish dish, and a vegetable dish. The meal is nicely ended with fresh fruit.

Here are some simple suggested menus for four:

(1)   *Rice*
      Barbecued spare-ribs
      Steamed asparagus

(2)   *Rice*
      Roast pork
      Chow Chinese cabbage

(3)   *Rice*
      Red-cooked chicken
      Peas

(4)   *Rice*
      Sweet-and-sour fish
      Chow broccoli

(5)   *Rice*
      Beef and mushrooms
      Tossed salad*

The meal would, of course, be rounded out with the usual extras such as shrimp chips to go with cocktails, a proper wine to accompany the main course, fruit for dessert, and tea with possibly a delicate wafer to end the meal.

For six people, I suggest starting with a soup course and increasing the amounts of the other courses or adding another dish to the suggested menus for four. The hostess should plan on using different methods of cooking for each dish. She should have, say, soup, rice, a braised dish, a roasted dish, and a stir fried dish which can be done at the last minute. For the novice I always advise against having more than one stir fried dish per meal. It is very difficult indeed to cook

* I mean a traditional American salad; a menu doesn't necessarily have to be 100% Chinese.

two stir fried dishes in succession and get both to the table piping hot.

One should avoid repetition in the menu. If you have beef in one dish, don't use beef again in your second dish; try pork or seafood. Vary textures in your menu. Don't have two diced dishes or two shredded dishes. How much more interesting to have one dish diced and the other shredded.

Here are some suggested menus for dinner for six:

(1) *Watercress soup*
 Rice
 Diced shrimp with vegetables
 Steamed spare-ribs with black bean sauce
 Cold cucumber salad Chinese style

(Soup and salad can be done ahead of time and spare-ribs may be started 15 minutes before shrimp-and-vegetable dish)

(2) *Bean curd soup*
 Rice
 Red-cooked beef
 Cold Chinese chicken salad
 Chow green beans

(All courses can be done ahead of time except for the chow dish)

(3) *Summer melon soup*
 Rice
 Chow pork chops with lettuce, tomatoes, and onions
 Red-cooked chicken livers

(Soup and chicken livers can be prepared ahead of time; chow dish is done at last minute)

Preparation of foods, that is, all cutting and mixing should be done earlier in the day and only last-minute cooking and reheating should be left to the end.

In our home when I am entertaining from eight to six-

teen people, we always serve a Chinese buffet. It is perhaps
not the most ideal way to serve Chinese food but isn't it
better to entertain in the intimacy of your home than take
guests to a restaurant?

Although food is very important, one of the most pressing
duties, indeed if not the first duty, of a good hostess is to see
that her guests are comfortable and are enjoying themselves.
Therefore a large dinner party requires extreme care in planning of the menu and use of all electrical equipment such
as frying pans, dutch ovens, and warmer trays.

This book is written to make menu planning easy. Just
pick a recipe from each section, making certain there isn't any
repetition of textures or ingredients. Use all the methods of
cooking.

I have chosen one of my menus for 16 people and will
discuss in minute detail how I go about preparing for such an
evening. This should give the reader a bird's eye view of how
it is done.

Marinated baby abalone on sticks
Shrimp chips
Hot and sour soup
Rice
Red-cooked beef with eggs
Sliced lettuce and tomatoes
Cold Chinese cucumber salad with chunks of crabmeat
Lion's Head
Cold poached chicken with hoisin sauce and scallions
Steamed spare-ribs with black bean sauce
Almond junket with iced fruit cocktail
Petits fours
Tea or coffee

On the day before the party all the marketing is done.
Baby abalone comes canned ready to eat and shrimp chips
may be purchased ready made in New York's and San Francisco's Chinatown. Otherwise, shrimp chips may be fried in

oil and made a few days in advance. They should be stored in air-tight containers. Cans of abalone (you will need four or five cans) should be chilled and opened just before guests arrive.

On the evening before, the red-cooked beef is prepared. Nine eggs are hard boiled and peeled. After the beef is cooked, the eggs are added to the pot and both beef and eggs are left overnight in the sauce. Meanwhile the almond junket may be prepared and refrigerated along with cans of fruit cocktail. The meat balls for the Lion's Head are prepared, cooked, and refrigerated. The Chinese cabbage part of the dish may be washed, sliced, and refrigerated in water. (Some of the vitamins are lost this way but for such a project it saves time.) Spare-ribs are parboiled and refrigerated.

The next morning the beef and eggs are removed from the pot and set aside but not refrigerated. The sauce may be stored in the refrigerator for future use, leaving enough on top of stove to use for the evening dinner. The chicken is poached and set aside to cool. The sauce for the chicken is prepared and placed in a serving dish, covered with cellophane wrap, and refrigerated. The cucumber salad is prepared and refrigerated.

In the afternoon, the soup is prepared and the proper amount of rice is washed, water premeasured, and pot set on burner all ready to go. Just before guests arrive the chicken is chopped, arranged on a platter (perhaps garnished with parsley). The beef is sliced and the eggs quartered lengthwise. These are arranged on a platter lined with lettuce. The tomatoes are sliced and arranged on a bed of lettuce. All platters should be covered with cellophane wrap. Tomato platter should be refrigerated.

The Lion's Head meat balls should be placed in an electric dutch oven, deep fat fryer, or chafing dish. The Chinese cabbage is drained and placed on top of meat balls but the dish is not started. The dish is placed on the serving table or buffet. Meanwhile the sauce for the spare-ribs is prepared and the electric frying pan is hooked up filled with water to serve as a steamer. The rice is started and the cans of abalone are opened and placed in serving dishes.

As the first guest arrives, the rice should be steaming on the lowest flame. About half an hour before dinner is served, bring the water to boil in the electric frying pan and place spare-ribs in it. Simmer Lion's Head. Just before dinner is announced, the soup is reheated, placed in individual bowls or cups. These in turn are brought to the buffet and placed on the hot tray. The sauce for the beef is heated and placed in a little pitcher. All cold dishes are brought to the buffet. If you have help for the evening, the help can do all the last minute details. Dinner is served!

The following is a list of Chinese stores, specialty or super-markets which carry some or all of the items listed in the book. The ones with asterisks fill mail orders.

Arizona:
Phoenix Produce Company
202 South Third Street
Phoenix

Tang's Market
4102 North 24th Street
Phoenix

Soleng's
2320 South 6th Street
Tucson

California:
Co-op Shopping Centers
1414 University Avenue or
1550 Shattuck Avenue
Berkeley

U-Save Center Market
1654 University Avenue
Berkeley

Yee Sing Chong Company*
950 Castelar Street
Los Angeles

Wing Chong Company*
367 Eighth Street
Oakland

S. P. Depot Market
310 "I" Street
Sacramento

Mow Lee Shing Kee Company*
774 Commercial Street
San Francisco

Illinois:
Man Sun Wing Company
2229 Wentworth Avenue
Chicago

Massachusetts:
Tai Kwong Company
60 Beach Street
Boston

Michigan:
Lun Yick Company
1339 Third Avenue
Detroit

New York:
Oriental Food Shop*
1302 Amsterdam Avenue
New York 27

Eastern Trading Company, Inc.*
2801 Broadway
New York 25

Wing Woh Lung
50 Mott Street
New York

Ohio:
Sun Lee Yuen Company
1726 Payne Avenue
Cleveland

Oregon:
Fong Chong Company
301 N.W. Fourth Avenue
Portland

Texas:
Oriental Import-Export Company*
2009 Polk Street
Houston

Taiwan Importing Company*
1716 Texas Avenue
Houston 2

Adler's*
2012 Broadway
San Antonio

Washington:
Wah Young Company*
416 Eighth Avenue South
Seattle

Thriftway Super Market
Villa Plaza
Tacoma

Ken's Super Market
9132 Veterans Drive
Tacoma 99

Washington, D.C.
Mee Wah Lung Company*
608 H Street, N.W.
Washington

INDEX

Abalone, 35–36
 on menu, 166
Aburage (Fried Bean Curd), 36–37, 80
Acorn Squash, Steamed, 101–2
"Aginomoto" (Monosodium Glutamate), 11
Almond Cookies, 150
Almond Junket, 150
 on menu, 166, 167
Anise Pepper of China, 32
Apples, Honeyed, 151
Are Choy Har, 94–95
Asparagus, Chicken with, 85
 Chow Frozen, 53
 Pork with, 74
 Steamed, 102

Bacon, as ingredient. *See* specific recipes
Bak Jam Gai, 159
Bak Suey Yu, 158–59
Bamboo Shoots, 16–17
Barbecued Spare-ribs, 156
Basic Congee, 138–39
Bass, Sea, with Chinese Vegetables, 97–98
 Poached, 158–59
 Steamed, 109–10
 Steamed, with Mushrooms, 111
 Sweet-and-Sour, 98
 in Vegetables, Fried, 120–21
Bau Yu (Abalone), 35–36
Bead Molasses, 10–11, 28–29
Bean Curd, 36–37
 Beef with, 67
 Deep-Fried, 36–37, 80
 Fermented, 29
 Fried, 68
  Deep-, 36–37, 80
 with Pork and Vegetables, 80–81
 Pressed, 81
 Red, 30
 Red-Cooked, 116

Red-Cooked, with Oyster Sauce, 116–17
 Soup, 141
Bean Sauce. *See* Black Bean Sauce; Brown Bean Sauce
Bean Sprouts, 17
 and Peppers, Chow, 58
 Shrimp with, 94–95
Beans. *See* Black Beans; Green Beans
Beef, 59–67
 with Bean Curd, Ground, 67
 with Broccoli, 61–62
 in Brown Bean Sauce Noodles, 128
 with Celery, Shredded, 63
 with Chinese Vegetables, Cellophane Noodles, 65–66
 Congee, 139
 with Frozen Mixed Vegetables, Ground, 64–65
 with Green Peppers, Tomatoes, Onions, 62–63
 in Lion's Head, 156–57
 Marinades for, 60, 64, 103, 142
 Pearl Balls, 105
 Red-Cooked, 117, 119
  on menu, 166–68
 in Rice, 136
  Congee, 139
 with Snow Peas, 60
 with Soft Fried Noodles, 127
 Steamed Ground, 102–3
 Steamed, Pearl Balls, 105
 Steamed, with Tea Melon, 103
 with Tea Melon, 103
 with Tea Melon and Ginger, Shredded, 64
 and Vegetables, 52, 59–67
Belly Pork, 38
 Thrice-Cooked, 157–58
 Twice-Cooked, 82
Beverages, 145–48
Bird's Nest, 38
Bitter Melon, 17–18
 Pork with, 73–74

Black Bean Sauce, Spare-ribs with, 106–7
Black Beans, 34
Black Tea, 146
Blenders, use of, 47
Bok Choy (Chinese Cabbage), 18
Beef with, 61
Chow Young, 56–57
Bor Lor Gai Peen, 83–84
Bot Gok (Star Anise), 33
Bow Le Tea, 146
Boxed Noodles, 34
Braising, 41
See also Red-Cooked Foods; specific recipes
Broccoli, 19
Beef with, 61–62
Chow Frozen, 54–55
Pork with, 74
Sliced Fish with, 97–98
Brown Bean Sauce, 28
Chicken with, 89–90
Noodles, 128
Brussels Sprouts, Chow Frozen, 54
Butterfish, Steamed, 109–10
Butterfly Shrimp, 92–93

Cabbage
Chinese, 18
Beef with, 61
Chow, 56–57
Chow Frozen, 54
See also Celery Cabbage; Mustard Cabbage
Cake, Steamed Sponge, 112–13
Cantonese Egg Foo Young, 71
Cantonese Soft Fried Chow Mein, 126–27
Care Jup Har, 94
Carrots, Chow, 57
Cauliflower, Beef with, 61
Chow Frozen, 54
Caw Yuk, 157–58
Celery, Chow Frozen, 53
and Cucumbers, Cold Shredded, 128–29
Salad, Cold, 160
Shredded Beef with, 63
Celery Cabbage, Chinese, 18–19
Beef with, 61
Pork with, 74

Cellophane Noodles, 34
Ground Beef, Vegetables with, 65–66
Cha Quar (Tea Melon), 22
Cha Quar Jing Ngow Yuk, 103
Cha Quar Ngow Yuk Tse, 64
Cha Shew, 155
Cha Shew Chow Fun, 134–35
Cha Shew Lo Mein, 124
Chard, Swiss, Chow Frozen, 54
Chestnuts. See Water Chestnuts
Chicken, 83–91
with Asparagus, 85
Bones, Sweet-and-Sour, 90–91
with Brown Bean Sauce, 89–90
Congee, 140
in Corn Soup, 142
Curried, 86
Livers, in Egg Rolls, 153–54
Livers, Red-Cooked, 120
Marinades for, 107, 108
with Mushrooms, 84
with Oyster Sauce, 88–89
with Peanuts, 87–88
with Pineapple, 83–84
Poached, 159
on menu, 166, 167
Red-Cooked, 118–19, 120
and Rice, 137–38
Congee, 140
Salad, Cold, 160–61
with Soft Fried Noodles, 124, 127
in Soups, 129, 142
Steamed, 107–8
Stock, 11–12
Sweet-and-Sour Bones, 90–91
Three Flavors, 91
with Vegetables, Diced, 86–87
Wings, Red-Cooked, 120
Chinese Broccoli, 19
See also Broccoli
Chinese Cabbage, 18
Beef with, 61
Chow, 56–57
Chinese Celery Cabbage, 18–19
Beef with, 61
Pork with, 74
Chinese Chives, 19–20
Omelette of, 69–70
Chinese Deep-Fried Squab, 154
Chinese Mixed Vegetables, 58–59

Chinese Mustard Cabbage, 20
  pickled, 20–21
    Pork with, 76–77
    Soup with, 131
  Soup, 142
Chinese Oysters, 24
Chinese Parsley, 31
Chinese Vegetables. *See* specific vegetables
Chive Omelette, Chinese, 69–70
Chives, Chinese, 19–20
Choong (Scallions), 32
Chopping, 46–47
Chow (cooking method), 5–6, 12, 48–98
Chow Are Choy Lot Tzu, 58
Chow Bor Choy, 55
Chow Dow Jai, 55–56
Chow Dun, 69–70
Chow Har Ding, 96–97
Chow Hoong Lo Bak, 57
Chow Lung Har, 91–92
Chow Mein, Cantonese Soft Fried, 126–27
Chow Yu Kow, 98
Choy Doh (Knife), 8–9
  using, 42–47
Choy Sum (Young Chinese Cabbage), 18
  Chow, 56–57
Chuen Guen, 153–54
Chuen Guen Pei, 35
Chung Choy (Salted Turnip), 26–27
Chung Choy Jing Gee Yuk, 105
Chunk (cutting method), 46
Cilantro (Chinese Parsley), 31
Clams in Rice, Minced, 138
Cloud's Ears, 24–25
Cold Cucumber Salad, 160
Cold Noodles, 131–32
Congee, 138–40
  Basic, 138–39
  Beef, 139
  Chicken, 140
  Fish, 139–40
  Pork Chops in, 140
Cookies, Almond, 150
Cooking methods, 41
  Poaching, 158–59
  Red-Cooking (*Hoong Siu; Lo Suey*), 114–15

Stir Frying (*Chow*), 48–52
Wet Steaming (*Jing*), 99–101
See also specific foods
Coriander, Fresh, 31
Corn, Chow Frozen, 54
  Soup, 142
Cornstarch, 12, 52
Crabmeat, with Cold Noodles, 132
  for Cold Salad, 161
  with Fried Noodles, 127
  Scrambled Eggs with, 70
Cucumber Salad, Cold, 160
  on menu, 166, 167
Cucumbers and Celery, Cold Shredded, 128–29
Curried Chicken, 86
Curried Pork, 72–73
Curried Shrimp, 95–96
Cutting, 42–47
  Chopping, 46–47
  Chunk, 46
  Dicing, 46
  Shredding, 45–46
  Slicing, 42–45
  Utensils for, 8–9
Cutting Boards, 9

Daai Gow Choy (Leeks), 31–32
Darjeeling Tea, 146
Dark Soy. See *See Au*
Dates, Red, 26
Deep Frying, 41
  See also *Hoong Siu*; specific recipes
Desserts, 149–51
  Almond Cookies, 150
  Almond Junket, 150
  Honeyed Apples, 151
  Steamed Sponge Cake, 112–13
Diagonal Slicing, 44–45
Dicing, 46
  See also Chicken; etc.
Dow Fu (Bean Curd), 36–37
  See also Bean Curd
Dow Fu Kon (Pressed Bean Curd), 81
Dow Fu Ngow Yuk, 67
Dow Fu Pok (Fried Bean Curd), 36–37, 80
Dow Fu Pok Gee Yuk, 80
Dow Fu Tong, 141
Dow See (Black Beans), 34
Dow See Pai Quot, 106–7

Dragon's Well Tea, 147
Dried ingredients, 24–28, 32–34
Drinks, 145–48
Duck, with Potatoes, Braised, 161–62
  Sauce, 29
  with Soft Fried Noodles, 124–127
Duck's Eggs, Salted, 39
  in Congee, 138–39
  Steamed Ground Pork with, 106
  Steamed Lobster with, 112
  in Three Variety Eggs, 108
Dun Far Tong, 143
Dun Mein (Fresh Egg Noodles), 35
Dung Goo (Mushrooms), 25–26
  See also Mushrooms
Dung Quar (Winter Melon), 23–24
  Red-Cooked, 115

Egg Drop Soup, 143
Egg Foo Young, 71
Egg Noodles, 35
Egg Rolls, 153–54
  Wrappers for, 35
Eggs, 68–71
  Chive Omelette, 69–70
  with Crabmeat, Scrambled, 70
  Foo Young, 71
  Hundred-Year-Old, 38
    in Three Variety Eggs, 108
  Kiangsu Egg Dish, 68–69
  Red-Cooked, 119
    on menu, 166, 167
  Salted Duck's, 39
    in Congee, 138–39
    Steamed Ground Pork with, 106
    Steamed Lobster with, 112
    in Three Variety Eggs, 108
  Steamed, 108–9
  Three Variety, 108

Far Jiu (Anise Pepper of China), 32
Fermented Bean Curd, 29
Fish, 97–98
  Congee, 139–40
  Fried, with Vegetables, 120
  with Mushrooms, Steamed, 111
  Poached, 158
  Salted, 26
  Steamed, 109–11
  Sweet-and-Sour, 98
  with Vegetables, 97
  with Vegetables, Fried, 120

Five-Flavored Spice Powder, 33
Fon Care Lot Tzu Ngow, 62–63
Foo Yu (Fermented Bean Curd), 29
Fooh Jook, 37
Fooh Quar (Bitter Melon), 17–18
Fooh Quar Gee Yuk, 73–74
Frozen Vegetables, Chow, 53–54
  Ground Beef with, 64–65
Frying. *See* Chow; *Hoong Siu;* specific foods
Frying Pans, use of, 5
Fun See (Cellophane Noodles), 34, 66

Gai Ding, 86–87
Gai Fun, 137–38
Gai Jook, 140
Gai Yung Sook Mei, 142
Gar Lay Gai, 86
Gar Lay Gee Yuk, 72–73
Gar Lay Har, 95–96
Garlic, 12–14
Gee Choy (Seaweed), 27–28
Ginger Root, 14–15
Gong Yu Gee (Dried Scallops), 27
  in Congee, 138
Goon Mein (Boxed Noodles), 34
Gow Choy (Chinese Chives), 19–20
  Omelette with, 69–70
Green Beans, Chow String Beans, 55–56
  Chow Frozen Italian, 54
Green Peppers, and Bean Sprouts, Chow, 58
  Shrimp with, 95
  Tomatoes, Onions, Beef with, 62–63
Green Tea, 146, 147
Gum Jum (Lily Flowers), 25
Gung Bau Gee Ding, 89–90
Guy Choy (Mustard Cabbage), 20
Guy Choy Tong, 142
Guy Lon (Chinese Broccoli), 19
  See also Broccoli
Guy Lon Ngow, 61–62
Gwo Pei (Tangerine Peel), 33–34

Hahm Choy (Pickled Cabbage), 20–21
  See also Pickled Cabbage
Hahm Dun (Salted Duck's Egg), 39
  See also Salted Duck's Eggs

Hahm Dun Jing Gee Yuk, 106
Hahm Yu (Salted Fish), 26
Hai Chow Dun, 70
Hairy Melon (Summer Melon), 21–22
Soup, 143–44
Ham, as ingredient. *See* specific recipes
Red-Cooked Fresh, 118
Har Mei (Dried Shrimp), 28
See also Shrimp
Har Too Tzu, 152
Herbs, Dried and Powders, 32–33
Heung New Fun (Five-Flavored Spice Powder), 33
Ho See (Dried Oysters), 24
Ho See Soong, 77–78
Ho Yau (Oyster Sauce), 30
Ho Yau Dow Fu, 116–17
Ho Yau Gai, 88–89
Ho Yau Gee Yuk, 72
Hoisin Jheung, 29–30
Hoisin Sauce, 29–30
Honeyed Apples, 151
Hoong Jo (Red Dates), 26
Hoong Siu (cooking method), 114
Hoong Siu Dow Fu, 116
Hoong Siu Dung Quar, 115
Hoong Siu Yu, 120–21
Hors d'oeuvres,
Abalone, Marinated Baby, 166
Chicken Livers, Red-Cooked, 120
Chicken Wings, Red-Cooked, 120
Egg Rolls, 153
Pearl Balls, 105
Pork Sausage, 38
Shrimp Balls, 152
Shrimp, Butterfly, 92
Shrimp Chips, 164, 166
Shrimp Toast, 152
Spare-ribs, Barbecued, 156
Hot Oil, 67
Hundred-Year-Old Eggs, 38
in Three Variety Eggs, 108
Hung Yan Beng, 150
Hung Yan Dow Fu, 150

Ingredients, 10–39
Chinese, 15–39
Dried, 24–28, 32–34
Herbs, Spices, 32–34
Noodles, Wrappers, 34–35

Sauces, 28–31
Vegetables, 16–24, 31–32
Dried, 24–27
Italian Green Beans, Chow Frozen, 54

Jahm Bahn (Cutting Board), 9
Jar Chiang Mein, 128
Jasmine Tea, 146–47
Jee Yau (Bead Molasses), 10–11, 28–29
Jeen Dow Fu, 68
Jeet Quar (Summer Melon), 21–22
Jeet Quar Tong, 143–44
Jing (Wet Steaming), 99–113
Jing Dun, 109
Jing Gai, 107–8
Jing Lo Shun, 102
Jing Loong (Steamer), 99–101
Jing Lung Har, 111
Jing Ngow Yuk, 102–3
Jing Yu, 109–10, 111
Jing Yu Peen, 110
Jook, 138–39
Jook Soon (Bamboo Shoots), 16–17
Jow (Deep Frying). *See* specific foods
Jow Bok Opp, 154
Jow Har Kow, 152–53
Junket, Almond, 150
on menu, 166, 167

Kale,
Beef with, 61
Chow Frozen, 53
Kan Choy Ngow Yuk Tse, 63
Keemun Tea, 146
Kiangsu Egg Dish, 68–69
Kiung Po Gai, 87–88
Knives, Chinese, 8–9
using, 42–47
Kohlrabi, Beef with, 61
Kwangtung Chow Mein, 126–27
Kwangtung Yung Dun, 71

Ladles (*Siou Hok*), 5–6, 51
Lamb, Red-Cooked Leg of, 118
with Soft Fried Noodles, 127
Leeks, 31–32
Lemon Sole, with Chinese Vegetables, 98
Lettuce, Buns, 78

Fried Rice with, 75
Pork Chops with, 75
Lien Ngow (Water Lily Root), 23
Light Soy, 10, 30
Lily Flowers, 25
Lily Root, Water, 23
Lion's Head, 156–57
  on menu, 166–68
Livers, Chicken
  in Egg Rolls, 153–54
  Red-Cooked, 120
Lo Hon Ji, 59
Lo Shon Chow Gai, 85
Lo Suey (cooking method), 114–15
Lo Suey Dun, 119
Lo Suey Gee Yuk, 118
Lo Suey Ngow Yuk, 117
Lo Suey Yang Yuk, 118
Lobster,
  Cantonese, 91–92
  Noodles with, 127–28
  Steamed, 111
  Steamed, with Salted Egg, 112
Lop Chong (Sausage), 38–39
  with Steamed Ground Pork, 106
Lor Mei Jing Ngow Yuk, 105
Lung Har Chow Mein, 127–28
Lung Jing Tea, 147
Lychee Tea, 146–47

Ma Jheung (Sesame Paste), 30
Ma Yau (Sesame Oil), 34
Mar Tai (Water Chestnuts), 22–23
Marinades,
  for Beef, 60, 64, 103, 142
  for Chicken, 107, 108
  for Pork, 69, 72, 73, 77, 141
Meat. *See also* Beef; Pork; etc.
  Chopping of, 46
  with Cold Noodles, 132
  Patties, Steamed, 104
  Shredding of, 45
  Slicing of, 44
  with Soft Fried Spaghetti, 125
Mei Fun (Rice Sticks), 35
Mei Jing (Monosodium Glutamate), 11
Melon. *See* Bitter Melon; Summer Melon; Tea Melon; Winter Melon
Menu planning, 163–68

Mien See (Brown Bean Sauce), 28
  See also Brown Bean Sauce
Miso (Bean Mash), 28
Mok Ye (Cloud's Ears), 24
Molasses, Bead, 10–11, 28–29
Monosodium Glutamate, 11
Mou Goo Gai Peen, 84
Mou Goo Gee Yuk, 74
Mou Soo Yuk, 68–69
Mun (Braising), 41
  See also specific foods
Mushrooms, 25–26
  Chicken with, 84
  Pork with, 74
  Steamed Sea Bass with, 111
Mustard Cabbage, 20
  Pickled, 20–21
    Pork with, 76–77
    Soup with, 131
  Soup, 142

Ng Fah Yuk (Belly Pork), 38. *See also* Belly Pork
Ng Heung Fun (Five-Flavored Spice Powder), 33
Ngah Choy (Bean Sprouts), 17. *See also* Bean Sprouts
Ngow Yuk Fun, 136
Ngow Yuk Jook, 139
Ngow Yuk Soong, 65–66
Niw Goo Yuk, 78–79
Nom Yu (Red Bean Curd), 30
Noodles, 34–35, 122–32
  Boxed, 34
  Brown Bean Sauce, 128–29
  Cantonese Soft Fried Chow Mein, 126–27
  Cellophane, 34, 65–66
  Cold, 131–32
  Fresh Egg, 35
  Ground Beef with Cellophane, 65–66
  with Lobster, 127–28
  Roast Pork Soft Fried, 124
  Soft Fried, Cantonese, 126–27
  Soft Fried, Roast Pork, 124
  in Soup, One Order, 129
  in Soup, with Pickled Mustard Greens, 131
  in Soup, Yang Chow, 130
  Three-Flavored, 123–24
Nori (Seaweed), 27–28

Oil, 12
  Sesame, 34
  Szechuan, 67
Okra, Chow Frozen, 54
Omelette, Chinese Chive, 69–70
  Egg Foo Young, 71
One Chicken Three Flavors, 91
One Order Noodles in Soup, 129
Onions, as ingredient. *See* specific recipes
Oolong Tea, 146, 147
Oyster Sauce, 30
  Chicken with, 88–89
  Pork with, 72
  Red-Cooked Bean Curd with, 116–17
Oysters, Dried, 24
  Pork with, 77–78

Parsley, Chinese, 31
Pea Starch (Cellophane) Noodles, 34
  Ground Beef, Vegetables with, 65–66
Peanut Oil, 12
Peanuts, Chicken with, 87–88
Pearl Balls, 105
Peas, Beef and Snow, 60
  Chow Frozen, 53
  Shrimp with, 95
  Snow Peas, 21
    Beef and, 60
Pei Dun (Hundred-Year-Old Eggs), 38
  in Three Variety Eggs, 108
Peppers, and Bean Sprouts, Chow, 58
  Beef, Tomatoes, Onions with, 62–63
  Shrimp with, 95
Pickled Cabbage (Greens), 20–21
  Noodles in Soup with, 131
  Pork with, 76–77
Pike, with Chinese Vegetables, 97–98
Pineapple, as ingredient. *See* specific recipes
Poaching, 158–59
  Chicken, 159
  Sea Bass, 158–59
Porgy, Steamed, 109–10
Pork, 52, 71–79, 155–58.
  See also Noodles; Omelettes; Soup

Barbecued Spare-ribs, 156
Belly, 38
  Thrice-Cooked, 157–58
  Twice-Cooked, 82
with Bitter Melon, 73–74
Chops in Jook, 140
Chops with Lettuce, Tomatoes, Onions, 75
in Congee, 140
Curried, 72–73
with Dried Oysters, Vegetables, 77–78
in Egg Rolls, 153–54
Fried Noodles, 124
Fried Rice, 134–35, 137
in Jook, 140
with Lettuce, Tomatoes, Onions, 75
Lion's Head, 156–57
Lobster recipes with, 92–93, 112
Marinades for, 69, 72, 73, 77, 141
with Mushrooms, 75
with Oyster Sauce, 72
with Oysters, Vegetables, 77–78
Patties, Steamed, 104
with Pickled Cabbage, 76–77
Red-Cooked, 118
Roast, 155
  Fried Rice, 134–35, 137
  Soft Fried Noodles; Soup
  See also Noodles; Soup
with Salted Duck's Egg, Steamed, 106
with Salted Turnip, Steamed, 105
Sausage, 38–39, 106
Soft Fried Noodles, Roast, 124
Spare-ribs, Barbecued, 156
Spare-ribs, Black Bean Sauce, 106–7
Steamed, 104
  with Salted Duck's Egg, 106
  with Salted Turnip, 105
Sweet-and-Sour, 78–79
Thrice-Cooked, 157–58
Twice-Cooked, 82
Potatoes, Braised Duck with, 161–62
Preparation, methods of, 40–47
Pressed Bean Curd with Pork and Vegetables, 81

Red Bean Curd, 30
Red-Cooked Foods, 114–21

Bean Curd, 116
Bean Curd, Oyster Sauce, 116–17
Beef, 117
  on menu, 166–68
Chicken, 118–19, 120
Chicken Livers, 120
Eggs, 119
  on menu, 166–68
Fish in Vegetables, 120–21
Lamb, Leg of, 118
Pork, 118
Winter Melon, 115
Red Dates, 26
Rice, 133–40
  Beef Congee, 139
  Beef Cooked in, 136
  Chicken Congee, 140
  Chicken Cooked in, 137–38
  Clams in, 138
  Congee, 138–40
    Beef, 139
    Chicken, 140
    Fish, 139–40
    Pork Chops in, 140
  Fish Congee, 139–40
  Fried, with Bacon, Lettuce, Tomatoes, Onions, 35–36
  Fried, Roast Pork, 134–35
  Fried, Yang Chow, 137
  Pearl Balls, 105
  Pork Chops in Jook, 140
  Pork Fried, 134–35
  Sticks, 35
  Wine, 11, 145
  Yang Chow Fried, 137
Roasting, 41
  See also specific meats
Rolling-Diagonal Slicing, 45

Sake, 145
Salads, 160–61
  Cold Chicken, 160–61
  Cold Cucumber, 160
  on menu, 166, 167
Salt, use of, 12
Salted Duck's Eggs, 39
  in Congee, 138–39
  Steamed Ground Pork with, 106
  Steamed Lobster with, 112
  in Three Variety Eggs, 108
Salted Fish, 26

Salted Turnip, 26–27
  Steamed Pork with, 105
Sam Jup Mein, 123–24
Sam Wong Dun, 108
Sang Chau (Light Soy), 10, 30
Sang Choy Bau, 78
Sauces, 10–11, 28–30
Sausage, Pork, 38–39
  with Steamed Ground Pork, 106
Scallions, 32
Scallops, Dried, 27
  in Congee, 138
Schools of cooking, 40–41
Sea Bass, with Chinese Vegetables, 97–98
  Poached, 158–59
  Steamed, 109–10
  Steamed, with Mushrooms, 111
  Sweet-and-Sour, 98
  in Vegetables, Fried, 120–21
Seasonings. *See* Ingredients
Seaweed, 27–28
See Au (Dark Soy), 10, 30
See Au Gai, 118–19
See Au Gai Gone, 120
See Au Gai Yick, 120
Sesame Butter, 30
Sesame Oil, 34
Sesame Paste, 30
Shark's Fin, 39
Shee Jai Opp, 161–62
Sherry, 11, 145
Shew (Roasting), 41
  See also specific meats
Shew Pai Quot, 156
Shiang Gur Nyuk Tzu, 81
Shiitake (Mushrooms), 25–26
  See also Mushrooms
Shredding, 45–46
Shrimp, 92–97
  Balls, 152–53
  with Bean Sprouts, 94–95
  Butterfly, 92–93
  Chips, 166–67
  in Cold Salad, 161
  Curried, 95–96
  Dried, 28
    in Congee, 138
  in Egg Rolls, 153–54
  with Soft Fried Noodles, 124, 127
  Toast, 152

with Tomato Sauce, 94
with Vegetables, Diced, 96–97
Shu Mei, 104
Shuen Choy (Pickled Cabbage), 20–21
   See also Pickled Cabbage.
Shuen Choy Gee Yuk, 76–77
Shuen Lot Tzu Tong, 144
Shuen Moy Jheung (Duck Sauce), 29
Siou Hok (Ladle), 5–6, 51
Siu Choy (Celery Cabbage), 18–19
   See also Celery Cabbage
Slicing, 42–45
   Diagonal, 44–45
   Rolling-Diagonal, 45
   Straight, 44
Snow Peas, 21
   Beef and, 60
Soft Fried Chow Mein, Cantonese, 126–27
Soft Fried Noodles, Roast Pork, 124
Soft Fried Spaghetti, 125
Sole, with Chinese Vegetables, 98
   Steamed Sliced, 110
Soot Dow (Snow Peas), 21
Soot Dow Ngow, 60
Soup, 141–44
   Bean Curd, 141
   Chinese Mustard Cabbage, 142
   Corn, 142
   De Luxe, Yang Chow Noodles in, 130
   Egg Drop, 143
   Noodles in, 129–31
   One Order Noodles in, 129
   with Pickled Mustard Green, 131
   Summer Melon, 143–44
   Sour and Hot, 144–45
   Yang Chow Noodles in, 131
Sour and Hot Soup, 144–45
Soy Sauce, 10–11, 30
   for Red Cooking, 114–15ff.
Spaghetti, Soft Fried, 125
Spare-ribs, Barbecued, 156
   with Black Bean Sauce, 106–7
   on menu, 166–68
Spices, Dried and Powdered, 32–33
Spinach, Chow, 55
   Chow Frozen, 53
Sponge Cake, Steamed, 112–13
Squab, Chinese Deep-Fried, 154

Squash, Acorn, Steamed, 101–2
Zucchini Soup, 144
Star Anise, 33
Steamed Dishes, 99–113
   Acorn Squash, 101–2
   Asparagus, 102
   Beef, 102–3
   Beef Balls, 105
   Beef with Tea Melon, 103
   Chicken, 107–8
   Eggs, 108–9
   Fish, 109–11
   Lobster, 111–12
   Lobster with Salted Egg, 112
   Meat Patties, 104
   Pearl Balls, 105
   Pork Patties, 104
   Pork with Salted Egg, 106
   Pork with Salted Turnip, 105
   Sea Bass with Mushrooms, 111
   Spare-ribs with Black Bean Sauce, 106–7
   Squash, 101–2
   Three Variety Eggs, 108
Steamers, 99–100
   Aluminum, 99
   Bamboo, 99
   Makeshift, 100
Stewing. *See* Red-Cooked Foods
Stir Frying. *See Chow* (cooking method)
Stock, Chicken, 11–12
Storage of ingredients, 16–39
Stores, list of, 169–70
String Beans, Chow, 55–56
   Chow Frozen, 54
Subgum   Jheung   (Ten-Flavored Sauce), 30
Sugar, use of, 12
Summer Melon, 21–22
   Soup, 143–44
Sweet-and-Sour Chicken Bones, 90–91
Sweet-and-Sour Fish, 98
Sweet-and-Sour Pork Cubes, 78–79
Swiss Chard, Chow Frozen, 54
Szechuan Oil, 67

Tangerine Peel, 33–34
Tea, 145–48
Tea Melon, 22

Beef with, 103
Shredded Beef with, 64
Ten-Flavored Sauce, 30
Thick Soy, 10–11, 28–29
Three-Flavored Noodles, 123–24
Three Variety Eggs, 108
Thrice-Cooked Pork, 157–58
Tiem Jook, 37
Tiem Shuen Gai Gwot, 90–91
Tiem Shuen Yu, 98
Toast, Shrimp, 152
Tomatoes, as ingredient. *See* specific recipes
Tse Jee Tao, 156–57
Turbot, Steamed Sliced, 110
Turkey Salad, Cold, 161
Turners (*Wok Chan*), 5–6, 51
Turnip, Salted, 26–27
Steamed Pork with, 105
Twice-Cooked Pork, 82
Tzu Sat Jing, 58–59

Utensils, 4–9
Cutting Boards, 9
Knives, 8–9
Ladles, 5–6, 51
Rice Pots, choosing of, 133
Steamers, 99–100
Turners, 5–6, 51
Woks, 4–5

Vegetable Oil, 12
Vegetables, 16–24
Chow-cooked, 49–59
Cutting of, 43–46
Frozen, use of, 53–54, 64–65
with Meats. *See* Beef; Pork; etc.
See also specific vegetables

Water Chestnuts, 22–23
Water Lily Root, 23
Wei Goon Nyuk, 82
Wet Steaming, 99–113
Wine, 11, 145
Winter Melon, 23–24
Red-Cooked, 115
Wok Chan (Turner), 5–6, 51
Woks, 4–5, 51–52
Seasoning of, 6–8
Wonton Pei, 35
Wonton Wrappers, 35
Wor Teap Har, 92–93
Wrappers, Egg Roll, 35
Wonton, 35
Wun Ye (Cloud's Ears), 24–25

Yang Chow Chow Fun, 137
Yang Chow Fried Rice, 137
Yang Chow Noodles in Soup De Luxe, 130
Yang Chow Wo Mein, 130
Yat Gai Sam Mei, 91
Yat Gaw Mein, 129
Yeen Sai (Chinese Parsley), 31
Yeen Wor (Bird's Nest), 38
Yellow Bean Sauce. *See* Brown Bean Sauce
Young Lung Har, 112
Yts Yow Tzu Mee, 131
Yu Chee (Shark's Fin), 39
Yu Jook, 139–40
Yu Peen, 97–98

Zucchini Soup, 144

K2